Ancient Civilizations

STUDENT WORKBOOK
California Reading Essentials and Study Guide

New York, New York   Columbus, Ohio   Chicago, Illinois

TO THE STUDENT

The *California Reading Essentials and Study Guide* accompanies the student textbook *Discovering Our Past: Ancient Civilizations*. This booklet is designed to help you use recognized reading strategies to improve your reading-for-information skills. For each section of the student textbook, you are alerted to key content and academic terms. Then, you are asked to draw from prior knowledge, organize your thoughts with a graphic organizer, and follow a process to read and understand the text. The *California Reading Essentials and Study Guide* was prepared to help you get more from your textbook by reading with a purpose.

Using this study tool will also help you learn the California standards for World History and Geography: Ancient Civilizations. The standards that apply to a given section are listed on the first page of that section.

 **Glencoe**

Send all inquiries to:
Glencoe/McGraw-Hill
8787 Orion Place
Columbus, OH 43240-4027

ISBN 0-07-870308-5

Printed in the United States of America

15 16 17 18 19 REL 13 12 11

Table of Contents

Table of Contents

World History and Geography: Ancient Civilizations Grade 6 Standards

WH6.1	**Students describe what is known through archaeological studies of the early physical and cultural development of humankind from the Paleolithic era to the agricultural revolution.**
WH6.1.1	Describe the hunter-gatherer societies, including the development of tools and the use of fire.
WH6.1.2	Identify the locations of human communities that populated the major regions of the world and describe how humans adapted to a variety of environments.
WH6.1.3	Discuss the climatic changes and human modifications of the physical environment that gave rise to the domestication of plants and animals and new sources of clothing and shelter.
WH6.2	**Students analyze the geographic, political, economic, religious, and social structures of the early civilizations of Mesopotamia, Egypt, and Kush.**
WH6.2.1	Locate and describe the major river systems and discuss the physical settings that supported permanent settlement and early civilizations.
WH6.2.2	Trace the development of agricultural techniques that permitted the production of economic surplus and the emergence of cities as centers of culture and power.
WH6.2.3	Understand the relationship between religion and the social and political order in Mesopotamia and Egypt.
WH6.2.4	Know the significance of Hammurabi's Code.
WH6.2.5	Discuss the main features of Egyptian art and architecture.
WH6.2.6	Describe the role of Egyptian trade in the eastern Mediterranean and Nile valley.
WH6.2.7	Understand the significance of Queen Hatshepsut and Ramses the Great.
WH6.2.8	Identify the location of the Kush civilization and describe its political, commercial, and cultural relations with Egypt.
WH6.2.9	Trace the evolution of language and its written forms.

Standards

WH6.3	**Students analyze the geographic, political, economic, religious, and social structures of the Ancient Hebrews.**
WH6.3.1	Describe the origins and significance of Judaism as the first monotheistic religion based on the concept of one God who sets down moral laws for humanity.
WH6.3.2	Identify the sources of the ethical teachings and central beliefs of Judaism (the Hebrew Bible, the Commentaries): belief in God, observance of law, practice of the concepts of righteousness and justice, and importance of study; and describe how the ideas of the Hebrew traditions are reflected in the moral and ethical traditions of Western civilization.
WH6.3.3	Explain the significance of Abraham, Moses, Naomi, Ruth, David, and Yohanan ben Zaccai in the development of the Jewish religion.
WH6.3.4	Discuss the locations of the settlements and movements of Hebrew peoples, including the Exodus and their movement to and from Egypt, and outline the significance of the Exodus to the Jewish and other people.
WH6.3.5	Discuss how Judaism survived and developed despite the continuing dispersion of much of the Jewish population from Jerusalem and the rest of Israel after the destruction of the second Temple in A.D. 70.

WH6.4	**Students analyze the geographic, political, economic, religious, and social structures of the early civilizations of Ancient Greece.**
WH6.4.1	Discuss the connections between geography and the development of city-states in the region of the Aegean Sea, including patterns of trade and commerce among Greek city-states and within the wider Mediterranean region.
WH6.4.2	Trace the transition from tyranny and oligarchy to early democratic forms of government and back to dictatorship in ancient Greece, including the significance of the invention of the idea of citizenship (e.g., from *Pericles' Funeral Oration*).
WH6.4.3	State the key differences between Athenian, or direct, democracy and representative democracy.
WH6.4.4	Explain the significance of Greek mythology to the everyday life of people in the region and how Greek literature continues to permeate our literature and language today, drawing from Greek mythology and epics, such as Homer's *Iliad* and *Odyssey*, and from *Aesop's Fables*.

WH6.4.5	Outline the founding, expansion, and political organization of the Persian Empire.
WH6.4.6	Compare and contrast life in Athens and Sparta, with emphasis on their roles in the Persian and Peloponnesian Wars.
WH6.4.7	Trace the rise of Alexander the Great and the spread of Greek culture eastward and into Egypt.
WH6.4.8	Describe the enduring contributions of important Greek figures in the arts and sciences (e.g., Hypatia, Socrates, Plato, Aristotle, Euclid, Thucydides).

WH6.5	**Students analyze the geographic, political, economic, religious, and social structures of the early civilizations of India.**
WH6.5.1	Locate and describe the major river system and discuss the physical setting that supported the rise of this civilization.
WH6.5.2	Discuss the significance of the Aryan invasions.
WH6.5.3	Explain the major beliefs and practices of Brahmanism in India and how they evolved into early Hinduism.
WH6.5.4	Outline the social structure of the caste system.
WH6.5.5	Know the life and moral teachings of the Buddha and how Buddhism spread in India, Ceylon, and Central Asia.
WH6.5.6	Describe the growth of the Maurya empire and the political and moral achievements of the emperor Asoka.
WH6.5.7	Discuss important aesthetic and intellectual traditions (e.g., Sanskrit literature, including the *Bhagavad Gita*; medicine; metallurgy; and mathematics, including Hindu-Arabic numerals and the zero).

WH6.6	**Students analyze the geographic, political, economic, religious, and social structures of the early civilizations of China.**
WH6.6.1	Locate and describe the origins of Chinese civilization in the Huang-He Valley during the Shang Dynasty.
WH6.6.2	Explain the geographic features of China that made governance and the spread of ideas and goods difficult and served to isolate the country from the rest of the world.
WH6.6.3	Know about the life of Confucius and the fundamental teachings of Confucianism and Daoism.
WH6.6.4	Identify the political and cultural problems prevalent in the time of Confucius and how he sought to solve them.

Standards

WH6.6.5	List the policies and achievements of the emperor Shi Huangdi in unifying northern China under the Qin Dynasty.
WH6.6.6	Detail the political contributions of the Han Dynasty to the development of the imperial bureaucratic state and the expansion of the empire.
WH6.6.7	Cite the significance of the trans-Eurasian "silk roads" in the period of the Han Dynasty and Roman Empire and their locations.
WH6.6.8	Describe the diffusion of Buddhism northward to China during the Han Dynasty.

WH6.7	**Students analyze the geographic, political, economic, religious, and social structures during the development of Rome.**

WH6.7.1	Identify the location and describe the rise of the Roman Republic, including the importance of such mythical and historical figures as Aeneas, Romulus and Remus, Cincinnatus, Julius Caesar, and Cicero.
WH6.7.2	Describe the government of the Roman Republic and its significance (e.g., written constitution and tripartite government, checks and balances, civic duty).
WH6.7.3	Identify the location of and the political and geographic reasons for the growth of Roman territories and expansion of the empire, including how the empire fostered economic growth through the use of currency and trade routes.
WH6.7.4	Discuss the influence of Julius Caesar and Augustus in Rome's transition from republic to empire.
WH6.7.5	Trace the migration of Jews around the Mediterranean region and the effects of their conflict with the Romans, including the Romans' restrictions on their right to live in Jerusalem.
WH6.7.6	Note the origins of Christianity in the Jewish Messianic prophecies, the life and teachings of Jesus of Nazareth as described in the New Testament, and the contribution of St. Paul the Apostle to the definition and spread of Christian beliefs (e.g., belief in the Trinity, resurrection, salvation).
WH6.7.7	Describe the circumstances that led to the spread of Christianity in Europe and other Roman territories.
WH6.7.8	Discuss the legacies of Roman art and architecture, technology and science, literature, language, and law.

World History and Geography: Medieval and Early Modern Times
Grade 7 Local Options

WH7.1	**Students analyze the causes and effects of the vast expansion and ultimate disintegration of the Roman Empire.**
WH7.1.1	Study the early strengths and lasting contributions of Rome (e.g., significance of Roman citizenship; rights under Roman law; Roman art, architecture, engineering, and philosophy; preservation and transmission of Christianity) and its ultimate internal weaknesses (e.g., rise of autonomous military powers within the empire, undermining of citizenship by the growth of corruption and slavery, lack of education, and distribution of news).
WH7.1.2	Discuss the geographic borders of the empire at its height and the factors that threatened its territorial cohesion.
WH7.1.3	Describe the establishment by Constantine of the new capital in Constantinople and the development of the Byzantine Empire, with an emphasis on the consequences of the development of two distinct European civilizations, Eastern Orthodox and Roman Catholic, and their two distinct views on church-state relations.

WH7.7	**Students compare and contrast the geographic, political, economic, religious, and social structures of the Meso-American and Andean civilizations.**
WH7.7.1	Study the locations, landforms, and climates of Mexico, Central America, and South America and their effects on Mayan, Aztec, and Incan economies, trade, and development of urban societies.
WH7.7.2	Study the roles of people in each society, including class structures, family life, warfare, religious beliefs and practices, and slavery.
WH7.7.3	Explain how and where each empire arose and how the Aztec and Incan empires were defeated by the Spanish.
WH7.7.4	Describe the artistic and oral traditions and architecture in the three civilizations.
WH7.7.5	Describe the Meso-American achievements in astronomy and mathematics, including the development of the calendar and the Meso-American knowledge of seasonal changes to the civilizations' agricultural systems.

READING ESSENTIALS AND STUDY GUIDE 1-1

Early Humans   *For use with pages 122–131*

Content Vocabulary

anthropologist: a scientist who studies how humans and their societies develop (page 123)

archaeologist: a scientist who digs up clues about the past (page 123)

artifact: a weapon, tool, or other item made by humans (page 123)

fossil: traces of plants or animals that have been preserved in rock (page 123)

nomad: a person who regularly moves from place to place (page 125)

technology: tools and methods that help humans perform tasks (page 126)

domesticate: to tame animals for human use (page 127)

specialization: a practice in which different people focus on different jobs (page 131)

Drawing From Experience

You know that certain jobs—computer technician, athlete, salesperson—often require traveling from place to place. But can you imagine an entire community that moved several times a year?

In this section, you will learn why bands of people once roamed the land—and what enabled them to finally settle down.

Organizing Your Thoughts

Use the following cause-and-effect chart to track how early humans adapted to their environment. Use details from the text to help you fill in each blank.

WH6.1 Students describe what is known through archaeological studies of the early physical and cultural development of humankind from the Paleolithic era to the agricultural revolution.

Focuses on:

WH6.1.1, WH6.1.2, WH6.1.3, WH6.2.9

Cause	Effect
1. Because people hunted and gathered . . .	. . . Paleolithic
2. Fire was a life-changing development because . . .	. . . fire provided
3. After people learned how to grow food . . .	. . . they were able to
4. Because not everyone was needed for farming . . .	. . . some people specialized

Early Humans (pages 123–126)

Main Idea Paleolithic people adapted to their environment and invented many tools to help them survive.

History is the story of our human past. Historians study and write about what people did long ago. Historians tell us that history began when people first began to write—about 5,500 years ago. The time before this is called *prehistory.* That is when the human story really begins.

Tools of Discovery Scientists study the earliest people and the things they left behind. One type of scientist is an **anthropologist.** These people study how different kinds of societies developed. They look for clues to how people related to one another. Other scientists called **archaeologists** hunt for clues to the past by digging underground. They choose sites where humans might once have settled. Archaeologists discover **artifacts,** such as tools, weapons, bowls, and other things humans made. They also hunt for **fossils,** or traces of plants or animals in rock.

Who Were the Hunter-Gatherers? Historians call the early period of human history the Stone Age. It is named for the fact that people during this time used stone to make tools and weapons. The earliest part of the Stone Age is the Paleolithic or Old Stone Age. This time began about 2.5 million years ago and lasted until around 8000 B.C.

We know that early humans spent most of their time searching for food. They hunted animals, caught fish, ate insects, and gathered nuts, berries, fruits, grains, and plants.

Because they lived off what the land provided, Paleolithic people were always on the move. They were **nomads,** or people who move regularly. They looked for good, rich land. They moved in bands of about 30. The group kept members safer.

At each new place, people camped near a stream or other water source. Women stayed close to the campsite.

READING ESSENTIALS AND STUDY GUIDE 1-1 (continued)

They cared for the children and searched nearby woods for berries, nuts, and grains.

Men had a different <u>task</u>. They hunted animals. This sometimes took them far from camp. Men had to learn the habits of different animals. They also needed to make tools for the kill. The earliest tools, such as clubs, were used for such a purpose. Men also killed animals by driving them off cliffs. Later, people invented spears, traps, and bows and arrows.

<table>
<tr><td>Academic Vocabulary</td></tr>
<tr><td>task: a piece of work (p. 125)</td></tr>
</table>

Adapting to the Environment The *way* Paleolithic people lived depended on *where* they lived. Those in warm climates needed little clothing or shelter. People in cold climates needed more. Many lived in caves. Over time, people created new kinds of shelters, such as animal hides held up by wooden poles.

Paleolithic people also learned to tame fire. Fire was important for many reasons. It provided warmth and light. It scared away wild animals. Food cooked over a fire tasted better, was easier to digest, and would keep longer. Archaeologists believe that fires were first started by rubbing two pieces of wood together and later with drill-like tools.

What Were the Ice Ages? Fire helped people survive the Ice Ages. From 100,000 B.C. to about 8000 B.C., thick ice sheets covered parts of Europe, Asia, and North America.

During the Ice Ages, people were at constant risk from cold and hunger. To survive, early humans had to adapt. People had to build sturdier shelters, make warmer clothing, and change their diets. Fire helped them live in this harsh environment.

Language, Art, and Religion Paleolithic people developed language. This made it easier for people to work together and pass on knowledge. Early people used both words and art. They made paint from crushed rocks. They painted animals on cave walls.

Some historians believe the early art could have had religious meaning or was meant to bring hunters good luck.

READING ESSENTIALS AND STUDY GUIDE 1-1 (continued)

The Invention of Tools Paleolithic people were the first to use tools and methods to help them perform tasks. This is called **technology.** Tools were made of a hard stone called flint. Flint would flake into sharp pieces when hit with a rock. By tying wooden poles to different shapes of flint, people made axes and spears.

Over time, early people made smaller and sharper tools—like fishhooks and needles—from animal bones. People used needles to make nets and baskets and to sew hides together for clothing.

5. How did the development of spoken language help Paleolithic people?

_____

_____

The Agricultural Revolution *(pages 127–131)*

Main Idea In the Neolithic Age, people started farming, building communities, producing goods, and trading.

After the last Ice Age ended, people began to change the way they lived. They learned how to **domesticate,** or tame animals. More control over animals meant more meat, milk, and wool. People also learned how to grow plants. People no longer had to roam from place to place in search of food. They could grow crops themselves. Gradually, farming replaced hunting and gathering.

These changes marked the beginning of the Neolithic Age. Also called the New Stone Age, this period lasted from about 8000 B.C. to 4000 B.C.

Why Was Farming Important? Historians call the Neolithic Age the farming <u>revolution</u>. The word *revolution* describes changes that affect many areas of life.

People scattered across the globe discovered how to grow crops at about the same time. What they grew depended on where they lived. The chart on the next page lists some of the crops grown in different parts of the world.

Academic Vocabulary
revolution: extreme complete change (p.127)

READING ESSENTIALS AND STUDY GUIDE 1-1 *(continued)*

Region	Crops
Asia	wheat, barley, rice, soybeans, millet, tea, sugarcane
Africa	coffee, yams, millet, barley, onions, wheat, flax
Europe	oats, rye, olives
Central and South America	beans, cotton, maize, tomatoes, squash, sweet potatoes, peanuts, potatoes, peppers, cocoa
North America	beans, sunflowers

The Growth of Villages Farming allowed people to stay in one place. Herders still drove their flocks wherever they could find grazing land. Farmers, however, had to stay put. They needed to water their plants and protect them from hungry animals. They also had to wait to reap the harvest. So they built permanent homes and created villages.

During the Neolithic Age, villages grew in Europe, India, Egypt, China, and Mexico. The earliest known communities have been found in the Middle East. One of the oldest is Jericho, which dates back to about 8000 B.C.

Another well-known Neolithic community is Çatal Hüyük in present-day Turkey. This village was home to about 6,000 people between 6700 B.C. and 5700 B.C. Some of its ruins have left behind clues to how its residents lived. For example, mud-brick houses were packed tightly together. People made wall paintings. They farmed, hunted, raised sheep and goats, worshiped together, and ate fish and bird eggs.

The Benefits of a Settled Life Neolithic people had a more secure life. Steady food supplies meant healthy, growing populations. Larger populations meant more workers to produce a bigger crop. Now they had a surplus to use for trade both within and outside their communities.

People made another advance in how they produced things. They began to practice **specialization,** or the development of different kinds of jobs. Now, not everyone needed to farm. So some people had time to develop other types of skills. These craftspeople made clay pottery and wove cloth. These workers then traded what they made for goods they needed.

READING ESSENTIALS AND STUDY GUIDE 1-1 (continued)

In late Neolithic times, toolmakers created better farming tools, such as the sickle used for cutting grain. In some places, people worked with metal. At first, they melted copper to make tools and weapons.

After 4000 B.C., craftspeople in western Asia made a discovery. They mixed copper with tin to make a stronger, longer-lasting metal called bronze. It became widely used between 3000 B.C. and 1200 B.C. This period is known as the Bronze Age.

6. Name two differences between people during the Paleolithic and Neolithic Ages.

_____

_____

READING ESSENTIALS AND STUDY GUIDE 1-2

Mesopotamian Civilization *For use with pages 132–139*

Content Vocabulary

civilization: complex societies (page 133)

irrigation: man-made way of watering crops (page 134)

city-state: city and its surrounding lands (page 135)

artisan: skilled worker who made various products (page 136)

cuneiform: ancient Sumerian form of writing (page 136)

scribe: record keeper (page 136)

empire: group of lands under one ruler (page 139)

Drawing From Experience

Doing a school project with a partner can be pretty simple. But what happens when you add a third, fourth— or tenth person to the group? Without structure and organization, things could get complicated.

In the last section, you learned why bands of people once roamed the land—and what enabled them to finally settle down. In this section, you will learn how early civilizations handled the need to organize their growing populations.

WH6.2 Students analyze the geographic, political, economic, religious, and social structures of the early civilizations of Mesopotamia, Egypt, and Kush.

Focuses on:

WH6.2.1, WH6.2.2, WH6.2.3, WH6.2.4, WH6.2.9

Organizing Your Thoughts

Use the following sequence chart to track the development of Mesopotamian civilization. Use details from the text to help you fill in the boxes.

Mesopotamia

Where: 1. _____

Climate: 2. _____

Farmers: 3. _____

Sumer

Government: 4. _____

Gods: 5. _____

Rulers: 6. _____

Classes: 7. _____

READING ESSENTIALS AND STUDY GUIDE 1-2 (continued)

Cradle of Civilization
Writing: 8. _____
Writers: 9. _____
Inventions: 10. _____
Math: 11. _____

Mesopotamia's Civilization (pages 133–136)

Main Idea Civilization in Mesopotamia began in the valleys of the Tigris and Euphrates Rivers.

Over thousands of years, some of the early farming villages developed into civilizations. **Civilizations** are complex societies. They have cities with different social groups and organized governments. Civilizations have art, religion, and a writing system.

Academic Vocabulary
complex: having many parts, details, ideas, or functions (p.133)

Why Were River Valleys Important? The first civilizations arose in river valleys. Near rivers, farming conditions were good. Rivers helped people travel and made trade easier.

As cities grew, they needed organization. People formed governments. Leaders took charge of food supplies, planned building projects, made laws, and formed armies. People did not worry so much about meeting basic needs. They developed religion and the arts. They invented ways of writing and created calendars.

The Rise of Sumer The earliest-known civilization arose in the Middle East on a flat plain between the Tigris and Euphrates Rivers. It was called Mesopotamia, which is Greek for "the land between the rivers."

Mesopotamia's climate was hot and dry. The rivers often flooded and left behind rich soil. However, flooding was unpredictable. It might flood one year, but not the next. Over time, farmers built dams and channels to control floods. They also built walls, waterways, and ditches to bring water to their fields. This way of watering crops is called **irrigation.** By 3000 B.C., many cities had formed in southern Mesopotamia in a region called Sumer.

READING ESSENTIALS AND STUDY GUIDE 1-2 (continued)

What Were City-States? Geographic features isolated Sumerian cities. Mudflats and desert made travel and communication difficult. Each Sumerian city—and the lands around it—became a separate **city-state.** Each city-state had its own government and did not belong to a larger unit.

Sumerian city-states often fought with each other. They went to war for glory and more territory. To ward off enemies, each city-state built a wall. First they mixed river mud with crushed reeds. Then they molded bricks and left them to dry in the sun. The hard, waterproof bricks were used for walls, homes, temples, and other buildings.

Gods and Rulers The Sumerians believed in many gods. Each god was thought to have power over a natural force or human activity, such as floods or basket weaving. The Sumerians built a grand temple called a ziggurat for their chief god. The word *ziggurat* means "mountain of god" or "hill of heaven." The ziggurat stood out as the centerpiece of the city. At the top was a shrine, or special place of worship. Only priests and priestesses could enter.

Priests and priestesses controlled much of the land. Some even ruled. Later, the government was run by kings who led armies and organized building projects. Eventually, the position of king became hereditary. That is, after a king died, his son took over.

What Was Life Like in Sumer? Sumerian kings lived in palaces. Ordinary people lived in small mud-brick homes. Most people farmed. Others were **artisans,** or skilled workers, and made metal products, cloth, or pottery. Other Sumerians worked as mechanics or traders. Merchants traded tools, wheat, and barley for copper, tin, and timber.

People in Sumer were divided into classes. The upper class included kings, priests, and government officials. The middle class included artisans, merchants, farmers, and fishers. The lower class included enslaved people who worked on farms or in temples. Slaves were prisoners of war, criminals, or those paying off debts.

In Sumer, women and men had separate roles. Men headed the households. Only males could attend school.

READING ESSENTIALS AND STUDY GUIDE 1-2 (continued)

Women, however, did have some rights. They could buy and sell property and run businesses.

12. What led to the isolation of each Sumerian city-state from others?

_____

_____

A Skilled People (pages 136–137)

Main Idea Sumerians invented writing and made other important contributions to later peoples.

The Sumerians' ideas and inventions were copied by other peoples. As a result, Mesopotamia has been called the "cradle of civilization."

Why Was Writing Important? The Sumerians' greatest invention was probably writing. Writing helps people keep records. Record keeping helps people pass their ideas on to others. Sumerian writing, called **cuneiform,** was developed to keep track of business deals. It <u>consisted</u> of wedge-shaped markings. With a sharp reed, these marks were cut into damp clay. Archaeologists have found thousands of cuneiform tablets. Mostly boys from wealthy families learned to write. After years of training, they became **scribes,** or record keepers. Scribes held honored positions in society. They often went on to become judges and political leaders.

Sumerian Literature The Sumerians also produced works of literature. The world's oldest known story is called the *Epic of Gilgamesh.* An epic is a long poem that tells the story of a hero. Gilgamesh is a king who travels around the world with a friend, performing great deeds. When his friend dies, Gilgamesh searches for a way to live forever, or immortality. He learns that immortality is only for the gods.

> **Academic Vocabulary**
>
> **consist:** what something is made up of (p.136)

READING ESSENTIALS AND STUDY GUIDE 1-2 (continued)

Advances in Science and Math The Mesopotamians' creativity also affected technology, mathematics, and time calculation. (See chart below.)

Mesopotamian Inventions

Technology	• irrigation system • wagon wheel • plow • sailboat
Mathematics	• geometry (to measure fields, put up buildings) • number system based on 60 (basis of today's 60-minute hour, 360-degree circle)
Time	• watched skies (to time crop planting and religious festivals) • recorded positions of stars and planets • developed 12-month calendar based on moon cycles

13. Of all Sumerian inventions, why is writing probably the greatest?

_____

_____

Sargon and Hammurabi (*page 139*)

Main Idea Sumerian city-states lost power when they were conquered by outsiders.

Over time, conflicts weakened Sumer's city-states. Now they were vulnerable to attacks from outsiders. One such enemy was the Akkadians of northern Mesopotamia.

The king of the Akkadians was named Sargon. In about 2340 B.C., Sargon conquered all of Mesopotamia. He set up the world's first empire. An **empire** is a group of many lands under one ruler. Sargon's empire lasted for more than 200 years before falling to invaders.

READING ESSENTIALS AND STUDY GUIDE 1-2 (continued)

In the 1800s B.C., a new group came to power in Mesopotamia. These people built the city of Babylon by the Euphrates River. Babylon quickly became a center of trade. Beginning in 1792 B.C., King Hammurabi of Babylon began conquering cities to the north and south. He created the Babylonian Empire.

Hammurabi is best known for his <u>code</u>, or collection of laws. This code covered crimes, farming, business activities, marriage, and the family. In fact, the code applied to almost every area of life. Many punishments in the Code of Hammurabi were cruel from our standpoint today. Still, his laws mark an important step toward a system of justice.

Academic Vocabulary
code: system of principles or rules (p. 139)

14. Why was the Code of Hammurabi an improvement over laws from individual city-states?

_____

_____

READING ESSENTIALS AND STUDY GUIDE 1-3

New Empires *For use with pages 142–147*

Content Vocabulary

province: political district (page 144)

caravan: group of traveling merchants (page 146)

astronomer: person who studies heavenly bodies (page 147)

Drawing From Experience

Suppose you were elected class president. How would you use your power?

In the last section, you learned how early civilizations handled the need to organize their growing populations. In this section, you will learn how two empires—the Assyrians and the Chaldeans—used power to focus on different aspects of their rule.

WH6.2 Students analyze the geographic, political, economic, religious, and social structures of the early civilizations of Mesopotamia, Egypt, and Kush.

Organizing Your Thoughts

Use the following chart to note characteristics of the Assyrian and Chaldean Empires. Use details from the text to help you.

	Assyrians	Chaldeans
Military	1.	4.
Government	2.	5.
Other contributions	3.	6.

The Assyrians (pages 143–144)

Main Idea Assyria's military power and well-organized government helped it build a vast empire in Mesopotamia by 650 B.C.

About 1,000 years after Hammurabi, a new empire arose—Assyria. The Assyrians lived near the Tigris River in fertile valleys. Outsiders liked the area, so the Assyrians built an army to defend their land. Around 900 B.C., they began taking over the rest of Mesopotamia.

Why Were the Assyrians So Strong? The Assyrian army was well organized. Its <u>core</u> group was made up of foot soldiers armed with spears and daggers. Other soldiers used their bow-and-arrow skills. Chariot riders and horsemen completed the Assyrian army.

Academic Vocabulary
core: the center or most important part (p. 143)

The army was the first to use iron weapons. Iron had been used for tools but was too soft for weapons. Then a people called the Hittites made iron stronger. They heated iron ore, hammered it, and then cooled it rapidly. The Assyrians learned this technique and made iron weapons.

The Assyrians were ferocious warriors. To attack cities, they tunneled under walls or climbed over them on ladders. They used tree trunks as battering rams to knock down city gates. Once they captured a city, the Assyrians carried away its people and goods and set the city afire.

The Assyrians punished anyone who resisted their rule. They drove people from their lands, brought in new settlers, and forced them to pay taxes.

A Well-Organized Government Assyrians needed strength to rule their large empire. By about 650 B.C., the Assyrian empire stretched east from the Persian Gulf to the Nile River in the west. Nineveh, on the Tigris River, was the capital.

Assyrian kings divided the empire into **provinces,** or political districts. They chose officials to govern each province. These officials collected taxes and enforced laws.

READING ESSENTIALS AND STUDY GUIDE 1-3 (continued)

The kings built roads to link the parts of their empire. Along the roadways were stations posted with government soldiers. These soldiers protected traders from bandits. Messengers on government business also stopped at the stations to rest and change horses.

Life in Assyria Assyrians were similar to other Mesopotamians. Their writing was based on Babylonian writing. They worshiped many of the same gods. Their laws were similar, but lawbreakers were more severely punished.

The Assyrians erected large temples and palaces filled with wall carvings. They wrote and collected literature. In fact, Nineveh had one of the world's first libraries.

7. Why were the Assyrian army's weapons so superior?

_____

_____

The Chaldeans (pages 145–147)

Main Idea The Chaldean Empire built important landmarks in Babylon and developed the first calendar with a seven-day week.

Assyria's cruel treatment of people led to rebellions. Around 650 B.C., the Assyrians began fighting each other over who would be king. A group called the Chaldeans rebelled. In 612 B.C., they captured Nineveh. Soon after, the Assyrian Empire crumbled.

The Chaldeans wanted to build an empire. By 605 B.C., led by King Nebuchadnezzar, they controlled nearly all of Mesopotamia.

The City of Babylon The Chaldeans rebuilt Babylon. Babylon quickly became the world's largest and richest city. A wall surrounded the city. Soldiers kept watch from towers built in the wall at 100-yard intervals.

In the center of the city stood large palaces and temples, including a huge ziggurat and an immense staircase

Academic Vocabulary

interval: space between things or time (p. 146)

READING ESSENTIALS AND STUDY GUIDE 1-3 (continued)

of greenery. Visible from any point in Babylon, it was the Hanging Gardens of King Nebuchadnezzar's palace. The garden had large trees, flowering vines, and other plants. A pump brought water from a nearby river.

A Greek historian described Babylon: "In magnificence, there is no other city that approaches it." Outside the city's center stood houses and marketplaces. There, artisans made pottery, cloth, baskets, and jewelry. They sold these to passing **caravans,** or groups of traveling merchants. Babylon lay on the major trade <u>route</u> between the Persian Gulf and the Mediterranean Sea. This ideal position helped it become rich from trade.

> **Academic Vocabulary**
>
> **route:** established course of travel (p. 146)

Babylon was also a center of science. Like earlier Mesopotamians, the Chaldeans thought it was important to pay attention to the skies. Changes in the heavens, they believed, revealed plans the gods had in store. They had specialists called **astronomers**—people who study heavenly bodies. These people mapped the stars, the planets, and the phases of the moon. The Chaldeans made one of the first sundials. They were also first to have a seven-day week.

Why Did the Empire Fall? As time passed, the Chaldeans's power began to slip away. They found it hard to control the peoples they had conquered. In 539 B.C. Persians from the mountains to the northeast captured Babylon. Mesopotamia became part of the new Persian Empire.

8. Name three contributions the Chaldeans made to society.

_____

_____

READING ESSENTIALS AND STUDY GUIDE 2-1

The Nile Valley *For use with pages 156–164*

Content Vocabulary

cataract: spot of rapid waters in a river (page 157)

delta: area of fertile soil at a river's end (page 157)

papyrus: a reed plant (page 160)

hieroglyphics: ancient Egyptian writing system combining picture and sound symbols (page 160)

dynasty: a line of rulers from one family (page 162)

Drawing From Experience

Suppose you and your family travel to a local state park for a weekend of camping. How would you decide where to pitch your tent?

In this section, you will learn why the earliest Egyptians settled along the banks of the Nile River.

Organizing Your Thoughts

Use the following organizer to note important facts about ancient Egypt. Use details from the text to help you fill in the table.

WH6.2 Students analyze the geographic, political, economic, religious, and social structures of the early civilizations of Mesopotamia, Egypt, and Kush.

Focuses on:

WH6.2.1, WH6.2.2, WH6.2.3, WH6.2.6, WH6.2.9

1. The Nile River	
2. Geographic Barriers	
3. Flooding	
4. Hieroglyphics	
5. Early Rulers	
6. Social Classes	

READING ESSENTIALS AND STUDY GUIDE 2-1 (continued)

Settling the Nile (pages 157–158)

Main Idea The Egyptian civilization began in the fertile Nile River valley, where natural barriers discouraged invasions.

Between 6000 B.C. and 5000 B.C., hunters and gatherers moved into the Nile River valley. They found the Nile green and fertile. They settled here, farmed the land, and built several villages. These people became the earliest Egyptians.

A Mighty River Since Egypt gets little rainfall, Egyptians had to rely on the Nile for water. They fished and bathed in the Nile. They used its water for farming, cooking, and cleaning.

The Nile flows north from the heart of Africa to the Mediterranean Sea, about 4,000 miles. This makes it the world's longest river. Traveling the Nile would be like going from Georgia to California and back again.

Two rivers meet to form the Nile: the Blue Nile in eastern Africa and the White Nile in central Africa. There, the water forms rapids called **cataracts.** Large ships cannot sail through the cataracts. So they can travel the Nile only for its last 650 miles.

A Sheltered Land In Egypt, the Nile runs through a narrow valley. Just before it reaches the Mediterranean Sea, it divides into different branches. These branches fan out over an area of rich soil. This fan is called a **delta.**

Deserts lie on both sides of the Nile Valley. To the west is part of the Sahara. It is the largest desert in the world. To the east is the Eastern Desert. It stretches to the Red Sea.

Because the deserts were so hot, the ancient Egyptians called them "the Red Land." These areas could not support human life. But they kept outside armies away from Egypt.

READING ESSENTIALS AND STUDY GUIDE 2-1 (continued)

Geographic <u>features</u> helped protect Egypt in other ways. To the south, dangerous cataracts blocked enemy boats. In the north were the delta marshes. Unfortunately, the people of Mesopotamia did not have geographic barriers. Mesopotamians constantly fought off attackers. Yet Egypt rarely faced these threats. As a result, Egyptian civilization grew and prospered.

Natural barriers did not completely close Egypt to the outside world. The Mediterranean Sea was to the north. Beyond the desert to the east was the Red Sea. These helped link Egyptians to trade outside its borders.

Within Egypt, people used the Nile for trade and transportation. Winds from the north pushed sailboats south. The flow of the Nile carried them north. This made Egypt different from Mesopotamia. There, city-states constantly fought each other. Egyptian villages, however, had friendly contact.

> **Academic Vocabulary**
>
> **feature:** shape or appearance of land or an object (p. 158)

7. Name a weakness and a strength of Egypt's desert lands.

_____

_____

The River People (pages 159–160)

Main Idea The Egyptians depended on the Nile's floods to grow their crops.

When the Tigris and Euphrates Rivers flooded, farmers irrigated their fields. However, the flooding was unpredictable. This made irrigation difficult.

Regular Flooding The Nile also flooded. However, these floods were more regular. Farmers did not have to worry that sudden overflows would destroy crops. Also, they did not have to worry that too little flooding would dry their fields.

READING ESSENTIALS AND STUDY GUIDE 2-1 (continued)

Water came to the Nile from rain and snow. Then from July to October, the Nile spilled over its banks. When the waters lowered, they left behind a layer of dark, rich mud.

How Did the Egyptians Use the Nile? The Egyptians became successful farmers. They planted wheat, barley, and flax seeds. Over time, they grew enough food to feed themselves and their animals.

They also used irrigation. To trap floodwaters, Egyptian farmers first dug basins, or bowl-shaped holes in the earth. Then they dug canals to carry water from the basins to the fields.

In time, Egyptian farmers built dikes, or earthen banks. These strengthened the basin walls. They developed other technology such as a *shadoof*, a bucket on a long pole. This would lift water from the river to the basins. They also developed geometry to *survey*, or measure, land.

Egyptians developed ways to use **papyrus.** This was a reed plant that grew along the shores of the Nile. They harvested papyrus to make baskets, sandals, river rafts, and later, paper.

What Were Hieroglyphics? The Egyptians used papyrus rolls as writing paper. Like the Mesopotamians, Egyptians developed their own system of writing. Called **hieroglyphics,** it was made up of thousands of picture symbols. Some symbols stood for objects and ideas. For example, to communicate the idea of a boat, a scribe would draw a tiny boat. Other symbols stood for sounds, like the letters of our own alphabet.

Some hieroglyphics conveyed public messages. Scribes carved these into stone walls and monuments. For everyday use, scribes invented a simpler script and wrote on papyrus.

In ancient Egypt, few people could read and write. However, some Egyptian men went to special schools in

Academic Vocabulary
technology: tools and methods used to help humans perform tasks (p. 159)

READING ESSENTIALS AND STUDY GUIDE 2-1 (continued)

temples. They studied reading and writing. They learned to become scribes, or record keepers. Eventually, they worked for the rulers, priests, and traders.

8. Why was irrigating their fields easier for Egyptians than for Mesopotamians?

_____

_____

A United Egypt (pages 161–162)

(Main Idea) Around 3100 B.C., Egypt's two major kingdoms, Upper Egypt and Lower Egypt, were combined into one.

Skillful farming led to more food than was needed, or a surplus. This freed some people to work as artisans instead of farmers. Artisans wove cloth, made pottery, carved statues, and shaped copper into weapons and tools.

Now Egyptians had goods to trade. First, they traded with each other. Then they traveled to Mesopotamia to trade. There, they may have picked up ideas about writing and government.

The Rise of Government Irrigation systems needed to be built and maintained. Grain had to be stored. Disputes over land needed to be settled. Gradually, government emerged.

The earliest rulers were village chiefs. A few strong chiefs united villages into small kingdoms. By 4000 B.C., Egypt was made up of two large kingdoms. Lower Egypt sat in the Nile delta. Upper Egypt lay in the south.

Egypt's Ruling Families About 3100 B.C., Narmer was king of Upper Egypt. He led his armies north and took control of Lower Egypt. Narmer ruled from Memphis, on the border

READING ESSENTIALS AND STUDY GUIDE 2-1 (continued)

between the two kingdoms. To symbolize the kingdom's unity, Narmer wore a double crown for both Upper and Lower Egypt.

Narmer's kingdom held together long after his death. His family passed power from father to son to grandson. This is called a **dynasty.**

Over time, ancient Egypt would be ruled by 31 dynasties for about 2,800 years. Historians group Egypt's dynasties into three main time periods—the Old Kingdom, the Middle Kingdom, and the New Kingdom. Each kingdom had a long period of strong leadership and stability.

9. In a dynasty, how do people decide who will become the next ruler?

_____

_____

Early Egyptian Life *(pages 163–164)*

Main Idea Egyptian society was divided into social groups based on wealth and power.

Different social groups in ancient Egypt looked like a pyramid. At the top of the pyramid sat the king. In the middle were the priests, nobles, traders, and artisans. On the bottom were the unskilled workers and farmers.

Egypt's Social Classes Egypt's upper class included nobles, army commanders, priests, and government officials. They lived in cities and on large estates along the Nile. Their homes were made of wood and mud bricks. Servants waited on them. They dressed in linen and wore makeup and jewelry.

Egypt's middle class included traders, artisans, and shopkeepers. They ran businesses or produced goods.

READING ESSENTIALS AND STUDY GUIDE 2-1 (continued)

They lived in smaller homes and dressed more simply. Artisans produced linen cloth, jewelry, pottery, and metal goods.

Farmers made up the majority of Egypt's population. Some farmers rented land and paid for their rent with crops. However, most farmers did not do this. They worked the land of wealthy nobles. Farmers lived in villages along the Nile. They had one-room huts and ate bread, beer, vegetables, and fruit.

City dwellers were unskilled workers who did physical labor. They unloaded cargo from boats, or made and stacked bricks. They lived in small mud-brick homes with dirt floors. Women dried fruit, made bread, and wove cloth on the flat rooftop of their homes.

Academic Vocabulary
labor: work that is physically hard (p. 164)

Family Life In ancient Egypt, the father headed the family. However, Egyptian women could own and pass on property, buy and sell goods, make wills, and get divorced. Upper-class women were in charge of temples and could perform religious ceremonies.

Few Egyptians sent their children to school. Mothers taught their daughters to sew, cook, and run a household. Boys learned farming or skilled trades from their fathers. Children played with board games, dolls, spinning tops, and leather balls.

10. Name the two types of farmers in Egypt's lower class and describe how they differed.

_____

_____

READING ESSENTIALS AND STUDY GUIDE 2-2

Egypt's Old Kingdom *For use with pages 165–170*

Content Vocabulary

pharaoh: Egyptian king (page 166)

deity: god or goddess (page 167)

embalming: mummy-making process (page 167)

mummy: body preserved by wrapping (page 168)

pyramid: mountainlike stone structure (page 168)

Drawing From Experience

What if everyone dropped to one knee when your principal walked down the hall at school? Or, what if the teachers obeyed his or her word without question?

In the last section, you learned why the earliest Egyptians settled along the banks of the Nile River. In this section, you will learn about the absolute power of the Egyptian pharaohs.

WH6.2 Students analyze the geographic, political, economic, religious, and social structures of the early civilizations of Mesopotamia, Egypt, and Kush.

Focuses on:
WH6.2.3, WH6.2.5

Organizing Your Thoughts

Use the following web to note Egyptian beliefs and the ways these beliefs affected their civilization.

1. Pharaohs
_____
_____

4. Life After Death
_____
_____

2. Religion
_____
_____

Egyptian Beliefs

3. Gods and Goddesses
_____
_____

5. Pyramids
_____
_____

READING ESSENTIALS AND STUDY GUIDE 2-2 (continued)

Old Kingdom Rulers *(page 166)*

Main Idea Egypt was ruled by all-powerful pharaohs.

The <u>period</u> known as the Old Kingdom began in Egypt around 2600 B.C. and lasted about 300 years. The Egyptians built cities and expanded trade. Their kings, or **pharaohs,** set up a government.

The pharaoh's word had to be obeyed without question. Pharaohs appointed officials who oversaw irrigation canals, grain houses, and crop planting. They also controlled trade and collected tax payments from farmers.

Egyptians served the pharaoh because they believed the kingdom's unity depended on a strong leader. They thought the pharaoh was the son of Re, the Egyptian sun god. Whenever the pharaoh appeared in public, people played music and bowed.

The pharaoh controlled Egypt's <u>welfare</u>. The pharaoh also performed rituals to benefit the kingdom. For example, the pharaoh drove a sacred bull around Memphis, Egypt's capital city. The Egyptians believed this would ensure good crops.

Academic Vocabulary
period: a portion of time in history (p. 166)

Academic Vocabulary
welfare: doing well; having what is needed to live well (p. 166)

6. Name two reasons why pharaohs were so powerful.

_____

_____

Egypt's Religion *(pages 167–168)*

Main Idea The Egyptians believed in many gods and goddesses and in life after death for the pharaohs.

Egyptians worshiped many **deities,** or gods and goddesses. They believed that these deities controlled the forces of nature and human actions.

The sun god, Re, was important because the sun was necessary for good harvests. Another god, Hapi, ruled the

READING ESSENTIALS AND STUDY GUIDE 2-2 (continued)

Nile River. Goddess Isis stood for loyal wives and mothers. She ruled over the dead with her husband, Osiris.

Life After Death Egyptians thought the dead went on a long journey. At the end, they came to a place of peace and plenty.

The *Book of the Dead* was a collection of spells and prayers. Egyptians studied this writing to reach life after death. They learned the spells and led good lives. They believed that the god Osiris would then grant them life after death.

For centuries, Egyptians believed that only the pharaohs and a few others could enjoy the afterlife. But the pharaoh's spirit needed a body. If his body decayed, his spirit would wander forever. If the pharaoh's spirit reached the next world, he would continue to care for Egypt.

To protect the pharaoh's body, the Egyptians developed a process called **embalming.** It included removing organs from the dead body, drying the body, filling it with spices and perfumes, sewing the body closed, cleaning it with oils, and tightly wrapping it in linen.

The wrapped body was known as a **mummy.** It was put in several wooden coffins. Then the pharaoh was ready for burial in a tomb.

Egyptian Medicine By embalming the dead, the Egyptians learned about the human body. Egyptian doctors used herbs and drugs to treat illnesses. They sewed up cuts and set broken bones.

Some doctors focused on treating specific parts of the body. These doctors were the first specialists in medicine. Egyptians also wrote the world's first medical books on scrolls of papyrus.

7. Why was Re the most important of the Egyptian gods?

_____

_____

READING ESSENTIALS AND STUDY GUIDE 2-2 (continued)

The Pyramids (pages 168–170)

Main Idea The Egyptians of the Old Kingdom built huge stone pyramids as tombs for their pharaohs.

For a pharaoh's tomb, Egyptians built gigantic **pyramids** made of stone. These <u>structures</u> protected the bodies from floods, wild animals, and grave robbers. They also held supplies that the pharaoh might need in the spirit world, including clothing, furniture, jewelry, and food.

Academic Vocabulary
structure: materials arranged to form a building or a statue (p. 168)

How Was a Pyramid Built? It took thousands of people many years to build a pyramid. Farmers, surveyors, engineers, carpenters, and stonecutters all worked on pyramids.

Each pyramid sat on a square base with a north entrance. To find true north, the Egyptians developed <u>principles</u> of astronomy. Using these principles, they also invented a 365-day calendar.

Academic Vocabulary
principle: law or fact of nature (p. 169)

Egyptians had to figure out the amount of stone and the angles for the walls. This advanced their mathematics. They invented a system of written numbers based on 10. They also created fractions.

Workers found the stone. Artisans cut the stone into blocks. Others tied the blocks to wooden sleds and pulled them to barges. The barges floated to the building site. There, workers unloaded the blocks, pushed them up ramps, and set them in place.

The Great Pyramid About 2540 B.C., the Egyptians built the Great Pyramid, about 10 miles from the modern city of Cairo. Built for King Khufu, it is one of three pyramids still standing in Giza. The Great Pyramid is 500 feet tall and has more than 2 million stone blocks.

8. Why did Egyptians preserve the bodies of their pharaohs?

_____

_____

READING ESSENTIALS AND STUDY GUIDE 2-3

The Egyptian Empire *For use with pages 178–186*

Content Vocabulary

tribute: forced payments (page 179)

Drawing From Experience

Every leader has an individual style. For example, one baseball coach might focus on good pitching and fielding. Another coach might prefer a team of power hitters.

In this section, you will learn how each pharaoh ruled Egypt during the Middle and New Kingdoms.

Organizing Your Thoughts

Use the following category chart to note how different rulers contributed to Egypt's New Kingdom.

WH6.2 Students analyze the geographic, political, economic, religious, and social structures of the early civilizations of Mesopotamia, Egypt, and Kush.

Focuses on:
WH6.2.3, WH6.2.5, WH6.2.6, WH6.2.7

Ahmose	1.
Hatshepsut	2.
Thutmose III	3.
Akhenaton	4.
Tutankhamen	5.
Ramses II	6.

READING ESSENTIALS AND STUDY GUIDE 2-3 (continued)

The Middle Kingdom (pages 179–180)

Main Idea The Middle Kingdom was a golden age of peace, prosperity, and advances in the arts and architecture.

The Middle Kingdom lasted from about 2050 B.C. to 1670 B.C. It was a golden age of <u>restored</u> stability, prosperity, and achievement.

The Drive for More Land During the Middle Kingdom, Egypt took control of new lands. Egyptian soldiers captured Nubia and attacked what is now Syria. The conquered peoples sent **tribute,** or forced payments, to the pharaoh. With the payment, pharaohs built dams, increased farmland, and built a canal between the Nile and the Red Sea.

The Arts Blossom During the Middle Kingdom, arts, literature, and architecture flourished. Painters covered tombs and temples with colorful scenes. Sculptors created large carvings of the pharaohs. Poets wrote works that praised the pharaohs.

Instead of building pyramids, pharaohs had their tombs cut into cliffs. This area became known as the Valley of the Kings.

Who Were the Hyksos? The Middle Kingdom ended as nobles plotted to seize power from the pharaohs. Egypt also faced invaders from western Asia—the Hyksos.

The Hyksos army was superior to the Egyptian army. The Hyksos rode horse-drawn chariots into battle. The Egyptians went on foot. Hyksos arms were made of bronze and iron. This made them stronger than the Egyptians' copper and stone weapons.

The Hyksos ruled Egypt for about 120 years. Then, around 1550 B.C., an Egyptian prince named Ahmose drove them out of Egypt.

7. Why were the Hyksos able to defeat the Egyptians?

_____

_____

Academic Vocabulary
restore: to put back into order or to fix (p. 179)

READING ESSENTIALS AND STUDY GUIDE 2-3 (continued)

The New Kingdom (pages 180–181)

Main Idea) During the New Kingdom, Egypt acquired new territory and reached the height of its power.

Ahmose's reign began a period known as the New Kingdom. From 1550 B.C. to 1080 B.C., Egypt grew richer and more powerful.

A Woman Ruler About 1473 B.C., a queen named Hatshepsut came to power. First, she ruled with her husband. After he died, she governed for her young nephew. Finally, she made herself pharaoh. Hatshepsut became the first woman to rule Egypt in her own right.

Hatshepsut was interested in trade more than conquest. During her reign, Egyptian traders exchanged wheat, metal tools, and paper for wood and furniture from the Phoenicians.

Egyptian goods were then traded by the Phoenicians to other people across the Middle East.

Expanding the Empire When Hatshepsut died, her nephew Thutmose III became pharaoh. Thutmose's armies expanded Egypt's borders north to the Euphrates River. His troops also regained control of Nubia, which had broken free from Egypt earlier.

Thutmose's empire grew rich. It claimed gold, copper, ivory, and other valuable goods from conquered peoples. Egypt also enslaved prisoners of war. These slaves were put to work building palaces, temples, and monuments. However, slaves could also own land, marry, and eventually gain their freedom.

8. What made Hatshepsut's rule different from that of her nephew Thutmose?

_____

_____

READING ESSENTIALS AND STUDY GUIDE 2-3 (continued)

Legacies of Two Pharaohs (pages 183–184)

Main Idea Akhenaton tried to change Egypt's religion, while Tutankhamen is famous for the treasures buried with him in his tomb.

About 1370 B.C., Amenhotep IV came to the throne. He and his wife, Nefertiti, tried to lead Egypt in a new direction.

A Religious Reformer The pharaohs were losing power to the priests. In an attempt to <u>maintain</u> his own power, Amenhotep started a new religion. People could worship only one god, called Aton. When the priests protested, Amenhotep removed many from their positions, seized their lands, and closed their temples. He changed his name to Akhenaton, or "Spirit of Aton." He began ruling Egypt from a new city.

Most Egyptians resisted Akhenaton's changes. They refused to accept Aton as the only god. Meanwhile, Akhenaton neglected his duties. He took no action when enemies attacked Egypt from what is now Turkey. These people were called the Hittites. Their invasion cost Egypt most of its lands in western Asia.

The Boy King When Akhenaton died, his son-in-law inherited the throne. The new pharaoh, Tutankhamen, was only 10 years old. He relied on help from palace officials and priests. He restored the old religion. After nine years, Tutankhamen died.

In 1922, Howard Carter, a British archaeologist, unearthed Tutankhamen's tomb. Besides the king's mummy, he found a gold mask of the pharaoh's face. Most royal tombs in Egypt had been looted by robbers. Carter's find enabled the boy king to capture people's imaginations. He became known as "King Tut."

> **Academic Vocabulary**
>
> **maintain:** to keep control of a situation (p. 183)

9. Why was Akhenaton's new religion so unpopular?

_____

_____

READING ESSENTIALS AND STUDY GUIDE 2-3 (continued)

The End of the New Kingdom (pages 184–186)

Main Idea Under Ramses II, Egypt regained territory and built great temples, but the empire fell by 1150 B.C.

Ramses II reigned for 66 years, from 1279 B.C. to 1213 B.C. During this time, Ramses regained lands in western Asia and constructed several new temples.

Academic Vocabulary
construct: to build or put together (p. 184)

Why Were Temples Built? Under Ramses II and other New Kingdom leaders, many temples rose throughout Egypt. Many were built by slaves. The most magnificent temple was Karnak at Thebes. Karnak has a huge hall that impresses visitors today.

Egyptian temples were different from modern churches, temples, and mosques. They did not hold regular services. Most Egyptians prayed at home. Temples were houses for the gods and goddesses. Priests and priestesses performed daily rituals there. They washed statues of the deities and brought them food.

The temples also served as banks. Inside, Egyptians stored valuables such as gold jewelry, sweet-smelling oils, and finely woven cloth.

Egypt's Decline and Fall After Ramses II, Egypt's power faded. Using strong iron weapons, groups from the eastern Mediterranean attacked Egypt by sea.

By 1150 B.C., Egypt had lost its empire. Starting in 900 B.C., one outside group after another ruled Egypt. The first conquerors were Libyans, who came from the west. In 750 B.C., the people of Kush, a land to the south, seized power. The Kush ruled Egypt for the next 80 years. Finally, in 670 B.C., Egypt was taken over by the Assyrians.

10. Why did Egyptians not use their temples for regular prayer services?

_____

_____

READING ESSENTIALS AND STUDY GUIDE 2-4

The Civilization of Kush *For use with pages 187–191*

Content Vocabulary

savanna: grassy plains in Africa (page 188)

Drawing From Experience

Think about your neighbors. Are some friendly and helpful? Are there other neighbors you wish would pack up and move away?

In this section, you will learn about how two of Egypt's neighboring civilizations cooperated—and clashed.

Organizing Your Thoughts

Use the following chart to note similarities and differences between the Kushites' capital cities of Napata and Meroë. Use details from the text to help you fill in each category.

WH6.2 Students analyze the geographic, political, economic, religious, and social structures of the early civilizations of Mesopotamia, Egypt, and Kush.

Focuses on:
WH6.2.6, WH6.2.8, WH6.2.9

	Napata	Meroë
Location	1.	5.
Expansion	2.	6.
Accomplishments	3.	7.
Decline	4.	8.

READING ESSENTIALS AND STUDY GUIDE 2-4 (continued)

Nubia (pages 188–189)

Main Idea) To the south of Egypt, the Nubians settled in farming villages and became strong warriors.

When Egyptians settled along the Nile, a civilization called Nubia arose. It was later known as Kush.

Cattle herders arrived in Nubia about 2000 B.C. The cattle grazed on **savannas,** or grassy plains. Later, people settled in farming villages, grew crops, and hunted with a bow and arrow. Soon the Nubians formed armies.

The Kingdom of Kerma More powerful Nubian kingdoms took over weaker ones. This created the kingdom of Kerma. The Egyptians traded cattle, gold, ivory, and slaves with Kerma. Egyptians also hired Nubian warriors to fight in their armies.

Kerma became a wealthy kingdom. Its artisans made fine pottery, jewelry, and metal goods. Like the pharaohs in Egypt, Kerma kings were buried in tombs that held precious stones, gold, jewelry, and pottery.

Why Did Egypt Invade Nubia? The Egyptian pharaoh Thutmose III invaded Nubia in the 1400s B.C. After a 50-year war, Kerma <u>collapsed</u>. The Egyptians seized much of Nubia and ruled it for the next 700 years.

During this time, the people of Nubia adopted Egyptian ways. They worshiped Egyptian gods and goddesses, worked with copper and bronze, and adapted Egyptian hieroglyphics to their own language.

Academic Vocabulary
collapse: to break down or cave-in completely (p. 189)

9. Why did the Egyptians like to trade with Kerma?

_____

_____

The Rise of Kush *(pages 189–191)*

Main Idea The people of Kush devoted themselves to ironworking and grew wealthy from trade.

> **Academic Vocabulary**
>
> **decline:** to move toward a lower level (p. 189)

As Egypt <u>declined</u> at the end of the New Kingdom, the Nubians broke away. By 850 B.C., a Nubian group had formed the independent kingdom of Kush. Powerful Kushite kings ruled from their capital city of Napata.

Napata sat along the upper Nile. There, trade caravans crossed the river. These caravans carried gold, ivory, valuable woods, and other goods from Kush to Egypt.

In time, Kush became strong enough to take control of Egypt. About 750 B.C., a Kushite king named Kashta headed north. He began the conquest of Egypt. His son Piye completed it in 728 B.C. Piye ruled both Egypt and Kush from Napata.

The kings of Kush built temples and monuments similar to those built by the Egyptians. The Kushites also built small pyramids in which to bury their kings.

The Importance of Iron Kush's rule over Egypt was short. During the 600s B.C., the Assyrians invaded Egypt. They drove the Kushites back to their homeland.

Kushites, however, gained something from the Assyrians—the secret to making iron. The Kushites became the first Africans to make iron. Soon, farmers in Kush could put iron in their plows instead of copper and stone. And they could grow more crops.

Kush's warriors also began using iron spears and swords. Traders from Kush carried iron products and enslaved peoples to Arabia, India, and China. In return, they brought back cotton, textiles, and other goods.

A New Capital In about 540 B.C., Kush's rulers moved to Meroë. Like Napata, the new capital was near the Nile River. But the rocky desert east of Meroë had iron ore. As a result, Meroë became an iron-making center.

READING ESSENTIALS AND STUDY GUIDE 2-4 (continued)

Kush's kings rebuilt Meroë to look like an Egyptian city. This included small pyramids, a grand avenue, and a huge temple.

Building a Profitable Trade Meroë became the center of a huge trading network throughout the Mediterranean and Indian Ocean areas. Kush's traders received leopard skins and valuable woods from the interior of Africa. They traded these, plus iron products and enslaved workers.

By the A.D. 200s, the kingdom began to weaken. As Kush declined, another kingdom called Axum took its place. Around A.D. 350, the armies of Axum burned Meroë to the ground.

10. Name two reasons why Kush became a wealthy kingdom.

_____

_____

READING ESSENTIALS AND STUDY GUIDE 3-1

The First Israelites *For use with pages 200–205*

Content Vocabulary

monotheism: belief in one god (page 201)

tribe: a separate family group (page 201)

Torah: a set of laws handed down from God to the Israelites (page 202)

covenant: agreement (page 202)

alphabet: a group of letters that stand for sounds (page 205)

Drawing From Experience

You may face tough decisions, such as: Should you reveal a secret to your best friend? Or, should you tell your math teacher that a friend is cheating? How do you decide what to do?

In this section, you will find out how the Israelites developed their ideas about right and wrong.

Organizing Your Thoughts

Use the following sequence chart to track the movement of the Israelites. Use details from the text to help you fill in the boxes.

WH6.3 Students analyze the geographic, political, economic, religious, and social structures of the Ancient Hebrews.

Focuses on:

WH6.3.1, WH6.3.2, WH6.3.3, WH6.3.4

Canaan

1. **Why Israelites settled here:** _____
2. **Religious beliefs:** _____
3. **Language:** _____

↓

Egypt

4. **Why Israelites came here:** _____
5. **Life in Egypt:** _____
6. **How they escaped:** _____

↓

Back to Canaan

7. **Where and from whom they got the Torah:** _____
   _____
8. **The Battle of Jericho:** _____

READING ESSENTIALS AND STUDY GUIDE 3-1 (continued)

The Early Israelites (pages 201–203)

Main Idea The Israelites believed in one God who set down moral laws for his people. They recorded their history in the Bible.

Around 1000 B.C., a people in southwest Asia built a kingdom in Canaan along the Mediterranean. They were the Israelites.

Who Were the Israelites? The Israelites focused their worship on only one God. This belief is called **monotheism.** Today, the Israelite faith is known as Judaism. The followers are known as Jews.

The Israelites spoke a language called Hebrew. They wrote down much of their history and religious beliefs. These records later became the Hebrew Bible.

The Israelites believed they were descended from a man named Abraham. The Hebrew Bible says that God told Abraham to lead his followers to Canaan. In return, God promised that Canaan would belong to Abraham and his descendants. Today, Lebanon, Israel, and Jordan occupy the land that was once Canaan.

Abraham had a grandson named Jacob who was also called Israel. In Canaan, Jacob raised 12 sons. His family was divided into **tribes,** or separate family groups. Later, these groups became known as the 12 tribes of Israel. The Israelites lived in Canaan for about 100 years. When a drought came, they left for Egypt.

From Slavery to Freedom In Egypt, the Israelites were enslaved by the pharaoh. He also ordered all Israelite baby boys to be thrown into the Nile River.

The Hebrew Bible says that one mother hid her baby. The pharaoh's daughter found him and named him Moses. When Moses grew up, he saw a burning bush. Then he heard a voice. He believed God was telling him to lead the Israelites out of Egypt to freedom.

According to the Hebrew Bible, God sent 10 plagues to trouble Egypt. A plague can mean "something that causes problems." The last of God's plagues killed all first-born

Academic Vocabulary
focus: center of interest (p. 201)

Academic Vocabulary
occupy: to live in or take possession of something (p. 201)

READING ESSENTIALS AND STUDY GUIDE 3-1 (continued)

children. However, most Israelite children were spared. The pharaoh set the Israelites free.

As they headed east out of Egypt, the pharaoh sent his army after them. According to the Hebrew Bible, God parted the Red Sea to let his people through. The Egyptians, however, drowned. Today, Jews remember this time with a holy day called Passover. Passover celebrates how the tenth plague "passed over" their homes.

What Are the Ten Commandments? On the way to Canaan, Moses climbed to the top of Mount Sinai. He received laws from God called the **Torah.** Later, they became the first part of the Hebrew Bible. The Torah described a **covenant,** or agreement, with God. God would return the Israelites to Canaan. In return, the Israelites would follow his laws. The Torah included the Ten Commandments.

The belief in only one God became the foundation for both Christianity and Islam. The Ten Commandments helped shape the laws of many nations.

9. What covenant was described in the Torah?

_____

_____

The Promised Land (pages 204–205)

Main Idea) The Israelites had to fight the Canaanites to return to their promised land.

It took 40 years to reach Canaan. After Moses died, Joshua took over. When the Israelites got to Canaan, they found Canaanites living there.

According to the Hebrew Bible, Joshua led the Israelites to the city of Jericho. He ordered them to march around the city walls. For six days, they did so, blowing trumpets. On the seventh day, Joshua ordered his people to raise a great shout. Then, the walls of Jericho crumbled.

Joshua led the Israelites in three more wars. The land they seized was divided among the 12 tribes.

READING ESSENTIALS AND STUDY GUIDE 3-1 (continued)

Who Were the Judges? After Joshua's death, the Israelites looked to judges for leadership. A judge was usually a military leader who commanded one or two tribes. Two judges were Deborah and Barak.

Deborah told Barak to attack the army of King Jabin, a Canaanite. In 1125 B.C., with Deborah's help, Barak and 10,000 Israelites destroyed King Jabin and his army.

The Israelites won control of central Canaan's hilly region. The Canaanites kept the coastal areas. The Israelites built walled towns. However, they looked to Canaan to <u>create</u> their alphabet and calendar.

Academic Vocabulary
create: to make (p. 204)

The Phoenician Alphabet The Phoenicians lived along the Mediterranean Sea. Through trade, the Phoenicians spread the idea of an **alphabet,** or a group of letters that stands for sounds. The alphabet made writing simpler and helped people keep records. The Phoenicians brought the alphabet to the Greeks. The Greeks passed it onto the Romans. Most Western alphabets are based on the Roman alphabet.

10. Where did the Israelites get their alphabet and calendar?

_____

_____

READING ESSENTIALS AND STUDY GUIDE 3-2

The Kingdom of Israel *For use with pages 206–212*

Content Vocabulary

prophet: person believed to be instructed by God to share his words (page 207)

empire: a nation that rules several other nations (page 209)

tribute: money or slaves given to a stronger ruler (page 209)

proverb: wise saying (page 209)

Drawing From Experience

What does the statement "united we stand, divided we fall" mean to you?

In the last section, you learned how the Israelites developed their ideas about right and wrong. In this section, you will learn what it meant to the 12 tribes of Israel.

Organizing Your Thoughts

Use the following chart to note events that occurred during the rule of the first Israelite kings. Use details from the text to help you.

WH6.3 Students analyze the geographic, political, economic, religious, and social structures of the Ancient Hebrews.

Focuses on:

WH6.3.2, WH6.3.3, WH6.3.4

1. Saul	
2. David	
3. Solomon	

The Israelites Choose a King *(page 207)*

Main Idea The Israelites chose a king to unite them against their enemies.

Around 1000 B.C., the Israelites feared the Philistines' power. They probably believed a king would unite them against the Philistines.

The Rule of King Saul In 1020 B.C., the Israelites asked a judge named Samuel to choose a king. Samuel was a **prophet**—someone who claims to be <u>instructed</u> by God. Samuel

Academic Vocabulary

instruct: to give knowledge or information (p. 207)

READING ESSENTIALS AND STUDY GUIDE 3-2 (continued)

believed that a king would tax the Israelites and make them slaves. Still, the Israelites chose a king, a warrior-farmer named Saul.

In battle after battle, Saul defeated the Israelites' enemies. However, the Hebrew Bible states that Saul displeased God by disobeying some of his commands. So God chose another king. In secret, Samuel anointed a young shepherd named David.

4. Why did the Israelites want a king?

_____

_____

David and Solomon (pages 209–210)

Main Idea **King David built an Israelite empire and made Jerusalem his capital city.**

According to the Hebrew Bible, a giant Philistine called out a challenge. His name was Goliath. He dared any Israelite to fight him one-on-one. David stepped forward. He held a shepherd's staff, a slingshot, and five stones.

Goliath rushed David with a spear. But David hurled one stone at the giant's forehead and killed him.

Saul put David in charge of the army. Israelite women sang praises of his victories. Saul plotted to kill David, so David hid until Saul and his three sons died in battle. He took the throne about 1000 B.C.

Once in power, according to the Hebrew Bible, David drove out the Philistines. He conquered other neighboring nations and created an **empire.** An empire is a nation that rules several other nations. Conquered peoples had to pay David **tribute.** Tribute is money or slaves given to a stronger ruler.

David made the Israelites pay taxes. He needed the money to expand Jerusalem and build a temple. David did not live to see the temple completed.

READING ESSENTIALS AND STUDY GUIDE 3-2 (continued)

The Rule of King Solomon When David died, his son Solomon became king and built the temple. It became the symbol and center of the Jewish religion.

In the Hebrew Bible, Solomon was known for his wise sayings, or **proverbs.** However, many Israelites hated his rule because of his taxes. The northern Israelites were especially unhappy. To raise more money, Solomon forced many of them to work in the mines.

When Solomon died, the northerners rebelled. Fighting broke out. In the north, ten of the 12 tribes set up their own nation, the kingdom of Israel with its capital of Samaria. In the south, the other two tribes founded the kingdom of Judah. Its capital was Jerusalem. Its people were called Jews.

5. Why did Solomon tax his people?

_____

_____

Academic Vocabulary
symbol: an item that represents an idea or a faith (p. 209)

A Troubled Time (pages 210–212)

Main Idea The Israelites were conquered and forced to leave Israel and Judah.

In southwest Asia, the Assyrians and Chaldeans were building empires. They wanted control of the trade routes that ran through Israel and Judah. Israel and Judah felt small and weak.

Who Were the Prophets? During this troubled time, the prophets wanted to bring the Israelites hope. They taught the importance of leading a moral life and helping others. They said that being faithful meant more than worshiping at a temple. It meant working for a just society. The Jewish goal of a just society also became an important goal of Christianity and Islam.

READING ESSENTIALS AND STUDY GUIDE 3-2 (continued)

What Caused the Fall of Israel? Everyone feared the war-like Assyrians. When they conquered a nation, the Assyrians destroyed buildings, scattered the people, and moved into the area.

In 722 B.C., the Assyrians conquered Israel and scattered the 10 tribes. Over time, the Israelites who were forced to move lost contact with those who remained in Israel and Judah. They are often called the "lost tribes of Israel."

The Assyrians brought in people from elsewhere to live in Samaria. These settlers mixed with the Israelites still there. A new culture developed, and the people became known as the Samaritans.

The Samaritans adopted many Israelite beliefs. They worshiped the God of Israel and followed the Israelites' religious laws. Over time, their religious practices developed separately. Today's Judaism developed from the religious practices of the tribes of Judah.

Why Did Judah Fall? In about 620 B.C., Judah was conquered by the Egyptians. Though they were able to keep their king, the Jews had to pay tribute to Egypt. However, in 605 B.C., the Chaldeans conquered Egypt. At first, the Chaldeans allowed the Jews to keep their king—as long as they paid tribute.

Several years later, the Jews and Egyptians united to rebel against the Chaldeans. In 597 B.C., the Chaldean King Nebuchadnezzar captured Jerusalem. He made 10,000 Jews leave the city and live in Babylon, the Chaldean capital. Then he appointed a new Jewish king.

In 586 B.C., the new king led a revolt against the Chaldeans. This time, the Chaldean ruler crushed Jerusalem and destroyed the temple. He sent thousands of Jews to Babylon, and this time was known as the Babylonian Captivity.

6. Why did the Assyrians and Chaldeans want to control Israelite land?

_____

_____

READING ESSENTIALS AND STUDY GUIDE 3-3

The Growth of Judaism *For use with pages 213–223*

Content Vocabulary

exile: forced life in a foreign land (page 214)

Sabbath: weekly day of rest and worship (page 214)

synagogue: Jewish house of worship (page 214)

Diaspora: Jews who lived outside Judaea (page 216)

messiah: a deliverer sent by God (page 221)

rabbi: teacher of the Torah (page 222)

Drawing From Experience

What do you do when you are unhappy? Do you wait for someone else to make things better? Or do you struggle to change things yourself?

In the last section, you learned what ideas of right and wrong meant to the 12 tribes of Israel. In this section, you will learn how different groups of Jews and their leaders reacted to being conquered and displaced.

WH6.3 Students analyze the geographic, political, economic, religious, and social structures of the Ancient Hebrews.

Focuses on:

WH6.3.2, WH6.3.3, WH6.3.4, WH6.3.5

Organizing Your Thoughts

Use the chart below to track details about the following people and places in Jewish history.

1. Babylon	
2. Judah	
3. The Diaspora	
4. The Maccabees	
5. King Herod	

READING ESSENTIALS AND STUDY GUIDE 3-3 (continued)

Exile and Return (pages 214–215)

Main Idea The Jews continued their religion during their exile in Babylon.

Jews called their years in Babylon an **exile.** This means they were forced to leave their homeland. During this time, the Israelite religion became Judaism.

Jews relied on their religion. They met on the **Sabbath**—their weekly day of rest and worship. People prayed, discussed their religion, and studied history. These meetings took place at **synagogues,** or Jewish houses of worship. Meeting together gave people hope.

Why Did Jews Return to Judah? During the 500s B.C., the Persians defeated the Chaldeans and took over Babylon. In 538 B.C., the Persian king Cyrus let the Jews return to Judah.

Though some Jews stayed in Babylon, many returned home. They rebuilt Jerusalem and the temple. Cyrus appointed officials to rule the country. He also collected taxes from the people.

Many scribes became Jewish leaders. A scribe named Ezra was in charge of writing out the five books of the Torah. The books were written on parchment and sewn together.

What Is in the Hebrew Bible? The Hebrew Bible is a <u>series</u> of 34 books collected together. The Torah, the Prophets, and the Writings that were added later make up the Hebrew Bible. Some of these books describe events in Jewish history. Others are books of poetry, literature, and proverbs.

Genesis is the first book of the Torah. It tells the story of Noah's ark. God had Noah build a giant ark, or boat, to hold his family and two of every animal in the world. Then he flooded the land to punish those who did not obey him. Genesis also explains why the world has many languages. The people of Babel tried to build a tower to heaven. God did not approve, so he made the people speak in different languages.

Academic Vocabulary

series: a number of things arranged in order and connected by being alike in some way (p. 215)

The Jews Look to the Future Parts of the Hebrew Bible describe God's plan for a peaceful future. In the book of Daniel, one story centers on Daniel, a king's adviser. Daniel refused to worship Babylonian gods. The Chaldeans threw him into a lion's den, but God protected him. This story was meant to remind Jews that God would rescue them.

The Jews believed that goodness would replace suffering and evil. Christians and Muslims also share this idea.

6. What helped the Jews survive their exile in Babylon?

_____

_____

The Jews and the Greeks (pages 215–216)

(Main Idea) Jews spread their beliefs to the Greek world and regained control of Judah.

In 331 B.C., Alexander the Great defeated the Persians. He had control of Judah, but he allowed the Jews to stay. Since Alexander loved all things Greek, he introduced the Greek language and ways to Judah.

What Was the Diaspora? At this time, Jews lived throughout Alexander's empire. Many still lived in Babylon. Some lived in Egypt and the Mediterranean. The scattering of Jews outside of Israel and Judah became known as the **Diaspora,** which meant "scattered."

Many Jews of the Diaspora learned the Greek language and ways. One group copied the Hebrew Bible into Greek. This <u>version</u> helped spread Jewish ideas throughout the Mediterranean.

Who Were the Maccabees? In 168 B.C., a Greek ruler named Antiochus controlled Judah. He made the Jews of Judah worship Greek gods and goddesses. A priest named Judas

Academic Vocabulary

version: a copy of writing which is in one's own language or style (p. 216)

READING ESSENTIALS AND STUDY GUIDE 3-3 (continued)

Maccabeus and his followers rebelled. They fled to the hills and formed an army known as the Maccabees.

After many battles, the Maccabees drove the Greeks out of Judah. They destroyed all <u>traces</u> of Greek gods and goddesses in their temple. Now, only the God of Israel could be worshiped there. Today, Jews remember this at a celebration called Hanukkah.

Academic Vocabulary
trace: very small amount (p. 216)

Priests from Judas Maccabeus's family became the new rulers of Judah. They led Judah to take back land that had been part of the kingdom of Israel.

7. How did Antiochus treat the Jews of Judah differently than Alexander treated them?

_____

_____

The Jewish Way of Life (pages 217–218)

Main Idea) Religion shaped the Jewish way of life.

Jewish laws affected daily life. They influenced education, food, and even their clothes. The laws reminded Jews of their religious responsibilities and focused on self-control. They also had to provide for the poor, visit the sick, do good deeds, give charity, and apply laws fairly.

Jewish Clothing Jewish law forbade mixing certain fabrics. Women used flax or wool to make cloth, but they could not combine the two.

Jewish men wore linen tunics. Some men layered another tunic on top. In cold weather, they added wool or sheepskin cloaks. Other items included caps, turbans, and sandals. Women wore long, simple dresses and shawls. Wealthy women wore leather shoes, makeup, and jewelry.

READING ESSENTIALS AND STUDY GUIDE 3-3 (continued)

Family Life Family was important to Jews and sons were especially valued. Sons carried on the family name, and after a father's death, they became head of the family.

Education was also important. Mothers were the first teachers. Fathers taught older sons how to earn a living and worship God. Later, elders took over boys' religious education and taught them the Torah. Religious teachers were community leaders.

Mothers taught their daughters at home. Here, girls learned to be wives, mothers, and housekeepers. They learned Jewish laws about food and clothing. They also learned about women of ancient Israel.

The Jewish Diet Under Jewish law, Jews could eat only certain animals like beef and lamb, but not pork. They could eat scaly fish, like salmon. But they could not eat shellfish or smooth-skinned fish, like eels. Laws about food were known as kashrut. This means "that which is proper."

Today, food prepared according to Jewish dietary laws is called kosher. Animals used in kosher meat must be killed in a certain way, inspected, salted, and soaked. Kosher Jews must not cook or eat milk products with meat.

In ancient times, everyday meals included fish, fruit, vegetables, and barley bread. Beverages were milk, water, wine, and beer.

8. Why were sons especially valued in Jewish society?

_____

_____

READING ESSENTIALS AND STUDY GUIDE 3-3 (continued)

The Jews and the Romans (*pages 220–223*)

Main Idea) Under Roman rule, the Jews were divided and rebellious. In response, the Romans destroyed the temple and exiled the Jews.

In 63 B.C., a people known as the Romans conquered Judah—which they renamed Judaea. The Roman capital lay far to the west in what is now Italy. So at first, the Romans allowed Jewish rulers to run Judaea.

The Rule of King Herod During this time, Judaea's most famous ruler was King Herod. He is known for the additions he made to the temple in Jerusalem.

Soon after Herod died, the Romans replaced the Jewish king with Roman officials. The Jews were divided over how to deal with the Romans. Different groups had different ideas about what they should do.

One group of Jews was the Pharisees, who taught the Torah. The Pharisees' classroom was the synagogue. They taught how to apply the laws of the Torah to daily life. This helped make Judaism a religion of the home and family. It also made the Pharisees popular among the common people.

Another group—the Sadducees—focused on how the Torah applied to priests. This is because most of the Sadducees were priests and scribes. This group did not agree with the Pharisees' teachings.

A third group—the Essenes—were priests who broke away from the Temple in Jerusalem. Many Essenes lived together in the desert. They spent their lives praying and waiting for God to rescue the Jews from the Romans.

In A.D. 1947, ancient scrolls were found in caves in the desert near the Dead Sea. Called the Dead Sea Scrolls, they have helped historians understand Judaism.

Jewish Revolts During the A.D. 60s, the Jews hated the Romans. They were waiting for a **messiah.** A messiah is a rescuer, sent by God. Other Jews known as Zealots did not want to wait for deliverance. They wanted to fight the Romans for their freedom.

In A.D. 66, the Zealots revolted against the Romans and drove them out of Jerusalem. Four years later, the Romans retook Jerusalem. They killed thousands of Jews. Others were forced to leave. The Romans also destroyed the temple in Jerusalem.

The Jews revolted again in A.D. 132. Three years later, the Romans crushed the rebellion. This time, the Romans forbade Jews to set foot in Jerusalem. They renamed Judah *Palestine.* This name refers to the Philistines whom the Israelites had conquered years before.

Jewish Teachers The Jews no longer had priests. Instead, leaders called **rabbis** taught the Torah.

One of the most famous rabbis was Yohanan ben Zaccai. After the revolt of A.D. 70, he founded a school in northern Palestine. For centuries, this was a center of Torah studies. Other rabbis also founded Torah schools. The rabbis wanted to save the Torah teachings and pass them on. They combined them in a book called the Talmud. The Talmud remains an important record of Jewish law.

For 2,000 years, most Jews lived outside of Palestine. They lived throughout the Mediterranean world. They even migrated to Southeast Asia, Central Europe, Russia, and the United States. In these places they made important contributions. They often faced hatred and persecution. In A.D. 1948, Palestine was divided. The new Jewish nation of Israel was created.

9. Why were the teachings of the Pharisees popular among the common people?

_____

_____

READING ESSENTIALS AND STUDY GUIDE 4-1

India's First Civilizations *For use with pages 238–245*

Content Vocabulary

subcontinent: a large mass of land; part of a continent but separate because of physical features like high mountains (page 239)

monsoon: strong winds that blow in one direction in the winter, and the opposite direction in the summer (page 239)

Sanskrit: the ancient written language of India (page 243)

raja: prince or tribal leader (page 243)

caste: social group that people are born into and cannot change (page 243)

guru: teacher for children of high-caste families (page 245)

Drawing From Experience

Where are the major cities in your state? Many large cities were built near rivers or other bodies of water that people could use for food and transportation.

In this section, you will learn how India's first civilization developed along the Indus River.

Organizing Your Thoughts

When the Aryans entered India, they changed it. Write some of the changes or inventions on the web below. Use details from the text to help you fill in each blank.

WH6.5 Students analyze the geographic, political, economic, religious, and social structures of the early civilizations of India.

Focuses on:

WH6.5.1, WH6.5.2, WH6.5.4, WH6.5.7

1. _____

2. _____

Aryan
changes or inventions

3. _____

4. _____

READING ESSENTIALS AND STUDY GUIDE 4-1 (continued)

The Land of India (pages 239–241)

Main Idea Climate and geography influenced the rise of India's first civilization.

India extends south from the continent of Asia. The Himalaya mountains separate India from the rest of Asia. This makes India a **subcontinent.** The Ganges and Indus Rivers are in India. The Ganges runs southeast into the Indian Ocean. The Indus flows southwest into the Arabian Sea. Their water comes from melting snow in the Himalayas. The Deccan Plateau is south of the Ganges and Indus River valleys. It is dry and hilly. The coastal regions have fertile plains.

India has **monsoons,** or strong winds. The winter monsoon blows in cold, dry air from the mountains. The summer monsoon brings warm, wet air from the Arabian Sea. Summer monsoons make the season rainy. If the rain comes on time, the crops will be good. If the rains are late, then there is a drought.

India's Early Civilization India's early civilization began in the Indus River valley where the floods create rich soil. The Harappa or Indus civilization lasted from about 3000 B.C. until 1500 B.C. Over 1,000 towns and cities stretched from the Himalaya to the Arabian Sea.

Harappa and Mohenjo-Daro Harappa and Mohenjo-Daro were large cities with about 35,000 people each. The cities had wide main streets and smaller side streets. Walls went around each neighborhood. And guards in fortresses protected the people.

Some houses were larger than others, but most were built with mud bricks. The houses had <u>similar</u> layouts with flat roofs, an open courtyard, wells, and indoor bathrooms. Pipes took wastewater to pits outside the city walls. Houses also had garbage chutes that led to bins in the streets. The government had to be well organized to do these things.

Academic Vocabulary
similar: having qualities or positions in common (p. 241)

READING ESSENTIALS AND STUDY GUIDE 4-1 (continued)

Harappan Society The Harappans left no written records. From the ruins, archaeologists learned that the royal palace and the temple were inside the fortress. This might mean that politics and religion were connected.

Most Harappans were farmers. They grew rice, wheat, barley, peas, and cotton. City dwellers made toys; clay pots; cloth; tools out of copper or bronze; and jewelry from gold, shells, and ivory.

The Harappans and the Mesopotamians began trading with each other about 2300 B.C. Some Harappan traders sailed across the Arabian Sea. Other traders traveled by land.

5. How is India separated from the rest of Asia?

_____

_____

The Aryans *(pages 242–243)*

Main Idea For the Indian civilization, new ideas and technology were developed.

About 1500 B.C., earthquakes destroyed Harappan cities. Also, the Indus River changed its course, flooding cities and farms. At about the same time, the Aryans moved into the river valley.

Who Were the Aryans? The Aryans were from central Asia. They had herds of cattle. Cattle were important for their meat, milk, and butter. The Aryans even used cattle as money. Individual wealth was measured by the number of cattle a person owned.

The Aryans were good warriors and expert horse riders and hunters. They had metal-tipped spears and wooden chariots. Sometimes they invaded nearby villages for food.

Academic Vocabulary
individual: a single member of a group (p. 242)

The Aryans left Asia about 2000 B.C. and crossed the Himalaya into India. They got to the Indus River valley around 1500 B.C. By 1000 B.C., the Aryans controlled northern India.

The Aryans Bring Change In India, the Aryans stopped living as nomads and became farmers. Over time, they said that cattle were sacred. People in India stopped eating cattle, or beef.

Aryan technology improved farming in India. The Aryans invented an iron plow and made iron tools. With these, they cleared India's rain forests, dug canals, and made the Ganges River valley good for farming. Farmers in north India grew wheat, barley, and a grain called *millet*. In the river valleys, farmers grew rice. In the south, they grew a mix of crops, including spices like pepper, ginger, and cinnamon.

The Aryans had not written things down when they were nomads. But when they became farmers, they invented a written language called **Sanskrit**. Using Sanskrit, they wrote down their sacred songs, poems, and prayers.

The Aryans lived in tribes ruled by a **raja,** or prince. Rajas often fought with each other over treasure, cattle, or women. These small kingdoms ruled from about 1500 B.C. to 400 B.C.

6. Why were the Aryans great warriors?

_____

_____

Society in Ancient India (pages 243–245)

Main Idea) The Aryans created a caste system that separated Indians into groups.

In India, a person was born into one social group, and could never change. This social group is known as a **caste**. The caste system had rules for almost everything a person did. Your caste dictated whom you married, your job, and your friends. India's society had thousands of castes, all tied to religion and tradition.

No one knows for certain why the Aryans invented the caste system. One reason could be that the Aryans had lighter skin than the Harappans. Another could be because it helped the Aryans keep control of the Harappans. There were a lot more Harappans, and the Aryans needed a way to keep people from revolting. They also needed to make people live by their rules.

Social Levels of the Caste System The thousands of different castes were grouped into four classes, or *varnas*. The top varna was the Brahmin. Brahmins were priests and could perform religious ceremonies.

The next varna was the Kshatriyas. These were warriors. They ran the government and the army. After the Kshatriyas came the Vaisyas, or "commoners." They were usually farmers and merchants. Then came the Sudras. They were manual laborers and servants with few rights. Most Indians were Sudras.

One group was too low to be part of the caste system—the Pariahs. *Pariah* meant "untouchable." Pariahs skinned animals and buried bodies. Most Indians believed that being near a Pariah was bad. So, Pariahs had to live apart from everyone else. When they traveled, Pariahs had to tap two sticks together. That way people would hear them coming and move away.

READING ESSENTIALS AND STUDY GUIDE 4-1 (continued)

The Role of Men and Women Grandparents, parents, and children all lived together with the oldest man in charge. This is called an extended family.

Men had many more rights than women. Usually, only sons could inherit property. Only men went to school or became priests. Women's education was done at home. Men had to have 12 years of schooling before they could marry. When they were young, boys studied with a **guru,** or teacher. When they were older, they went to schools in the cities.

Parents arranged marriages for their children, who were often as young as 13 years old. Divorce was not allowed. But if a couple could not have children, the husband could marry a second wife.

When a high-caste man died, his body was burned. Then his wife was supposed to throw herself into the flames. This is called *suttee.* If a widow did not die, it shamed the family.

7. What were the five major groups in Indian society?
   (*Hint:* four were castes, and one was below caste.)

   _____

   _____

READING ESSENTIALS AND STUDY GUIDE 4-2

Hinduism and Buddhism *For use with pages 246–253*

Content Vocabulary

Hinduism: one of the oldest religions in the world; has thousands of gods and goddesses that control the forces of nature (page 247)

Brahman: the universal spirit that is a main part of Hinduism (page 247)

reincarnation: the idea of living many different lives; an important belief in Hinduism (page 248)

dharma: divine law; requires people to perform duties of their caste (page 248)

karma: the consequences of how a person lives; if you live a good life, you have good karma (page 248)

Buddhism: a religion founded by Siddhartha Gautama (page 249)

nirvana: a state of wisdom achieved after giving up all desires (page 249)

theocracy: a government led by religious leaders (page 252)

Drawing From Experience

Does your family practice a religion? Many people follow their religion by going to a church, temple, or mosque.

In the last section, you learned how India's first civilization developed along the Indus River. In this section, you will learn about India's two main religions, Hinduism and Buddhism.

WH6.5 Students analyze the geographic, political, economic, religious, and social structures of the early civilizations of India.

Focuses on:

WH6.5.3, WH6.5.5

Organizing Your Thoughts

The Buddha said that people should follow the steps of the *Eightfold Path.* What are the steps of the path? Use details from the text to help you fill in the blanks.

1.	
2.	
3.	
4.	
5.	
6.	
7.	
8.	

Reading Essentials and Study Guide 4-2 (continued)

Hindusim (pages 247–248)

Main Idea) Hinduism grew out of the ancient beliefs of the Aryans.

Hinduism began with the religion of the Aryans. The Aryan religion had many deities who ruled nature. Over time, the Aryan religion added ideas from the Indian people to create Hinduism.

Early Hinduism Hindus believe in one universal spirit called **Brahman.** They also believe in thousands of deities that are a different part of Brahman.

The Upanishads are very old sacred texts. These writings talk about how each person looks for the universal spirit. They say our souls are like lumps of salt, and Brahman is a glass of water. When salt is put into water, it disappears. But the water is salty. Like salt, our souls disappear and become part of the universal spirit.

What Is Karma? Hindus believe that a soul eventually joins Brahman when a person dies. However, a soul must live many lives—even as an animal—before it joins Brahman. The idea of living many lives, one after another, is called **reincarnation.** It <u>affects</u> how Hindus live their daily lives and how they treat animals because they consider all life sacred.

If people do the duties of their caste, they will get a better next life. So they must follow **dharma,** or the divine law. It <u>requires</u> people to perform the duties of their caste. If you follow dharma, then you have good **karma.** Karma is the result of how a person lives. For example, if you live a good life and do your duty, you have good karma.

These beliefs in dharma and karma made people accept the caste system. A dedicated Hindu thinks that higher caste people really are better than lower caste people. The idea of reincarnation gave hope to everyone, including servants because they could be reborn in a higher caste in the next life if they did their duty.

Academic Vocabulary
affect: to make a change in or have an influence on (p. 248)

Academic Vocabulary
require: something that is necessary to do or to have (p. 248)

READING ESSENTIALS AND STUDY GUIDE 4-2 (continued)

9. How is karma related to reincarnation?

_____

_____

Buddhism (pages 249–253)

Main Idea A new religion, Buddhism, appealed to many people in India and other parts of Asia.

By 600 B.C., many Indians began to question Hindu ideas. They wanted a simpler, more spiritual religion for common people. They found this in the teachings of Buddha.

Who Is the Buddha? Prince Siddhartha Gautama was born about 563 B.C. He ruled a kingdom near the Himalaya. Today this <u>area</u> is in southern Nepal. He was wealthy, married, and had a son. One day he left the palace and saw beggars and people suffering. Siddhartha became <u>aware</u> of their circumstances. He asked himself why people suffered.

To search for answers, he left his family, lived alone, fasted, and meditated, or emptied his mind of thought. Legend says that Siddhartha meditated for 49 days. Then, he came to an understanding about life.

Siddhartha spent the rest of his life teaching people about his discovery. People called him the Buddha, which means "Enlightened One." His lessons about life and suffering are called **Buddhism.**

What Is Buddhism? The Buddha taught that there was one way to see truth in the world. Everyone should stop wanting fame, money, and worldly things. Then they would reach **nirvana,** or a state of wisdom.

The Buddha said that the only way to stop desiring things is to follow the Eightfold Path, which gives rules for living a good life. The Buddha believed in reincarnation—but with a difference. He thought that people could stop being reborn if they followed the Eightfold Path.

Academic Vocabulary
area: a space of land (p. 249)

Academic Vocabulary
aware: to have understanding or knowledge of something (p. 249)

READING ESSENTIALS AND STUDY GUIDE 4-2 (continued)

The Buddha did not accept the caste system. He thought that all people—even the lower castes—could reach nirvana. This made Buddhism very popular among the lower castes and the Pariahs. They, too, could escape suffering and find peace.

Buddhism in Southeast Asia The Buddha preached his ideas for more than 40 years. When he died, his disciples spread his message all over Asia.

Over time, the Buddhists split into two groups. The first was Theravada Buddhism. *Theravada* means "teachings of the elders." It says that the Buddha was a great teacher, but not a god. Theravada Buddhism spread south and east. It was adopted in what is now known as Sri Lanka in the 200s B.C. It also became popular in Indochina.

Mahayana Buddhism The second kind of Buddhism is *Mahayana* Buddhism. It says that Buddha is a god who came to save people. Mahayanas think people can go to heaven if they worship the Buddha. In heaven, they can follow the Eightfold Path to reach nirvana.

Mahayana Buddhists also honor the *bodhisattvas.* Bodhisattvas are enlightened people who do not go to heaven right away. They stay on earth to help others.

Mahayana Buddhism spread north into China, Korea, and Japan. In Tibet (in central Asia) it mixed with Hinduism and Tibet's own religions. This mix made a special kind of Mahayana Buddhism.

At that time, Tibet's Buddhist and government leaders were called *lamas.* When religious leaders also head the government, it is called a **theocracy.** The Dalai Lama led the government. The Panchen Lama led the religion. Both lamas were considered reincarnations of the Buddha.

Today, many Buddhists live in Thailand, Cambodia, and Sri Lanka. But very few live in India, where the Buddha first taught.

READING ESSENTIALS AND STUDY GUIDE 4-2 (continued)

What is Jainism? Buddhism did not survive in India. However, another religion developed. It was called Jainism. It challenged Hindu beliefs. Followers of Jainism believed that there were 24 saints. The greatest of these was Mahavira. He taught Jainism.

Followers of Jainism, called Jains, rejected the caste system of Hinduism. They also emphasized nonviolence, or ahimsa. Jains refuse to hurt any living thing—even insects. They believe all life is sacred.

Ahimsa's Impact Today The idea of ahimsa was long-lasting. Mohandas Gandhi, an Indian leader of the 1900s, used ahimsa. Gandhi and his followers led peaceful protests to help India gain its independence from Britain. Even in the United States, leaders have used ahimsa to bring about change. The most famous example of this was Martin Luther King, Jr. He led civil rights protests in the 1950s and 1960s.

10. How could a Buddhist reach nirvana?

_____

_____

Name_____ Date_____ Class_____

READING ESSENTIALS AND STUDY GUIDE 4-3

India's First Empires *For use with pages 259–267*

Content Vocabulary

dynasty: a series of rulers from the same family (page 260)

stupa: a Buddhist shrine shaped like a dome or mound (page 262)

pilgrim: a person traveling to a religious shrine or place (page 264)

WH6.5 Students analyze the geographic, political, economic, religious, and social structures of the early civilizations of India.

Focuses on:
WH6.5.6, WH6.5.7

Drawing From Experience

Think about cities where a lot of people visit—New York City; Orlando, where Disney World is; and San Francisco. Visitors, or tourists, spend a lot of money in those cities. This helps make those cities wealthy and gives people jobs.

In the last section, you learned about India's two main religions, Hinduism and Buddhism. In this section you will learn about the Maurya and Gupta empires. Their cities grew wealthy from trade and visitors.

Organizing Your Thoughts

The Maurya and Gupta empires made many contributions to India and the world. Fill in the chart below. Use details from the text to help you fill in each blank.

	Maurya Empire	**Gupta Empire**
Dates the empire was in existence	1.	5.
Capital city	2.	6.
Contributions	3.	7.
Religion	4.	8.

63

The Mauryan Dynasty (pages 260–262)

Main Idea The Mauryan dynasty built India's first great empire.

India began as many small kingdoms. India's princes fought over these small kingdoms for years. Then India became part of the Persian Empire and was invaded by Alexander the Great.

Who Built India's First Empire? While Alexander kept one part of India busy, Prince Chandragupta Maurya took over part of the Ganges River valley. When Alexander left, Chandragupta took over almost all of northern India.

In 321 B.C., Chandragupta founded the Mauryan **dynasty**—a series of rulers from the same family. He set up a centralized government in the capital city of Pataliputra. To keep control, Chandragupta also set up a strong army and a good spy system. He made a postal system for fast communication.

Emperor Asoka's Reign Many historians think that the Mauryan empire's greatest king was Asoka. Asoka ruled from about 273 B.C. to 232 B.C.

Asoka was a strong military leader who grew to hate war. After one bloody fight, he promised to dedicate his life to peace. He promised to follow the Buddha's teachings.

Asoka was the first great Buddhist king. He built hospitals for people and animals. He also built new roads with shelters and shade trees so travelers could rest.

Asoka sent many Buddhists out to teach Buddhism in India and Asia. In India, he had workers carve the Buddha's teaching on stones. He also had workers build thousands of **stupas,** or Buddhist shrines. Asoka allowed Hindus to remain Hindus.

When there is a good road system and a strong ruler, trade is good. Trade was very good under Asoka. India became the center of a trade network that stretched all the way to the Mediterranean Sea.

READING ESSENTIALS AND STUDY GUIDE 4-3 (continued)

The Fall of the Mauryan Empire Asoka died in 232 B.C. Unfortunately, the kings who followed him were not good leaders. The empire grew weak.

These kings made many bad decisions. They forced merchants to pay heavy taxes, but gave no services—like fixing the roads—in return. They took the peasants' crops, leaving people to starve. The people turned against the rulers. In 183 B.C., the last Mauryan king was killed by one of his own generals.

9. Why was Asoka an important ruler?

_____

_____

The Gupta Empire (page 264)

Main Idea) **The Gupta empire reunited much of northern India and became wealthy through trade.**

For the next 500 years, India had no strong ruler. Then a prince in the Ganges River valley rose to power. His name was Chandragupta, just like the founder of the earlier empire.

Chandragupta founded the Gupta dynasty in A.D. 320. He ruled from the old capital city, Pataliputra. When he died, his son Samudragupta took over. Samudragupta gained new lands for the empire until it covered almost all of northern India. The Guptas <u>dominated</u> northern India for almost 200 years.

Trade made the Gupta empire rich. People traded salt, cloth, and iron. The Gupta rulers controlled much of the trade. They also owned silver and gold mines, and large estates, or farms.

Trade created jobs. Cities grew along trade routes and were filled with inns and other places for travelers.

Merchants were not the only ones traveling. **Pilgrims**—people who travel to religious shrines or other holy places—used the trade routes. Cities with famous temples became rich because of pilgrims.

Academic Vocabulary
dominate: to have control over someone else (p. 264)

READING ESSENTIALS AND STUDY GUIDE 4-3 (continued)

The Guptas made Hinduism the official religion. They gave money to support Hindu scholars and shrines. The shrines often had sculptures inside them of deities.

Art and science developed during the Gupta empire. It was India's golden age.

10. How did the Gupta empire become wealthy?

_____

_____

Indian Literature and Science *(pages 265–267)*

Main Idea) The Mauryan and Gupta empires made important contributions in literature, mathematics, and science.

Artists, builders, scientists, and writers were busy under the Mauryan and Gupta empires.

India's Sacred Texts The *Vedas* of India are an ancient collection of sacred verses, hymns, prayers, and teachings. For a long time, they were part of India's oral tradition. An oral tradition is a group of stories and songs that are told aloud, but not written. When the Aryans invented Sanskrit, the Vedas were written down.

Other kinds of literature were written down, too. India has two very famous sacred texts: the *Mahabharata* and the *Ramayana*. These sacred texts tell about heroes and their deeds.

Both sacred texts have religious and moral lessons. Yet they are filled with excitement and danger. People enjoyed them.

Written about 100 B.C., the *Mahabharata* is a long sacred text. It is about a war to control an Indian kingdom. The best-known section is the Bhagavad Gita. That means

READING ESSENTIALS AND STUDY GUIDE 4-3 (continued)

"Song of the Lord." In it, the deity Krishna tells people that they should do their duty in battle, even when it is hard.

One of India's best-known authors was Kalidasa from the Gupta dynasty. He wrote plays, poems, love stories, and comedies. His poem *The Cloud Messenger* is a Sanskrit poem that describes the beautiful landscapes of India.

Music, Art, and Architecture Music was an important part of people's lives in India. Many early sacred texts were sung, and music was used in plays and at festivals. Tambourines, flutes, drums, and lutes were some of the musical instruments of the day.

What we know about early Indian art is mostly from religious stone sculptures that have survived. Indian statues and Indian architecture represented different Buddhist themes.

Indian Math and Science Aryabhata was the leading mathematician of the Gupta empire. He was one of the first to use algebra. Indian mathematicians invented the <u>concept</u> of infinity. Infinity is something that goes on without ending. They also invented the idea of zero, or nothingness, and the number symbols for 0, 1, 2, 3, 4, 5, 6, 7, 8, and 9.

Academic Vocabulary
concept: an idea or thought (p. 266)

At that time, people in Europe and the Middle East were using Roman numerals. Arab traders started using Indian numbers in the A.D. 700s. By the A.D. 1200s, people in Europe used these symbols.

Early Indians also invented algorithms. An algorithm is a series of steps that you follow to solve a problem. Today, computer programmers use algorithms.

Indian astronomers mapped the movements of the planets and stars. They knew that the earth was round and that it went around the sun. Indians also understood gravity.

READING ESSENTIALS AND STUDY GUIDE 4-3 (continued)

Gupta doctors set broken bones, performed operations, invented medical tools, and used herbs in treating illness. A doctor named Shushruta even did plastic surgery. Indian doctors thought that it was important to find the cause of a disease and not just cure it.

11. In what branches of science did ancient Indians make advances?

_____

_____

READING ESSENTIALS AND STUDY GUIDE 5-1

China's First Civilizations   *For use with pages 276–283*

Content Vocabulary

dynasty: a series of rulers from the same family (page 278)

aristocrat: nobles, or upper class people, whose wealth comes from their land (page 279)

pictograph: written characters that stand for objects (page 280)

ideograph: two or more pictographs that are joined together to represent an idea (page 280)

bureaucracy: appointed officials who take care of different parts of the government (page 281)

mandate: a formal command to rule or do something important (page 282)

Dao: the "Way," or a king's actions to keep the gods happy (page 282)

Drawing From Experience

How do we get the people who head our government? Our political leaders are elected. Then they appoint—or choose—people to help them. The appointed people are called bureaucrats. Bureaucrats help elected leaders run the government.

In this section, you will learn how geography helped shape China's civilization. You will also learn about the Shang dynasty that ruled China. You will learn that they had bureaucrats, too!

WH6.6 Students analyze the geographic, political, economic, religious, and social structures of the early civilizations of China.

Focuses on:
WH6.6.1, WH6.6.2

Organizing Your Thoughts

Many things were discovered during the Zhou dynasty. Use details from the text to help you name four of them.

1.	
2.	
3.	
4.	

READING ESSENTIALS AND STUDY GUIDE 5-1 (continued)

China's Geography (pages 277–278)

Main Idea Rivers, mountains, and deserts helped shape China's civilization.

The Huang He, or Yellow River, flows 2,900 miles across China. As it crosses the land, it picks up yellow dirt that turns the water yellow. Like the Nile, the Huang He flooded the land. This deposited rich soil in the river valley.

When the Huang He flooded, many people drowned. Farms were destroyed and millions of people starved. That is why the Chinese call the Huang He "China's Sorrow."

The Chang Jiang, or Yangtze River, is longer than the Huang He. It flows east across China to the Yellow Sea. The Chang Jiang valley also has good farmland.

Only about one-tenth of China can be farmed. The rest of the land includes mountains like the Himalaya, Kunlun Shan, or Tian Shan, or desert like the Gobi. For a long time, mountains and desert separated China from the rest of the world.

Over time, people in Chinese towns and cities united into one kingdom. They called it "the Middle Kingdom." The Chinese thought that it was the most important kingdom in the world and that they had the most knowledge.

5. Name two rivers that were important to early Chinese civilization.

_____

_____

READING ESSENTIALS AND STUDY GUIDE 5-1 (continued)

The Shang Dynasty (pages 278–281)

Main Idea Rulers known as the Shang became powerful because they controlled land and had strong armies.

Chinese civilization started near the Huang He. It had rich farmland, so there was plenty of food. People began building towns and cities there. China's first rulers were probably part of the Xia **dynasty,** a line of rulers who belong to the same family. Little is known about the Xia. More is known about the the Shang. The Shang kings ruled from about 1750 B.C. to 1045 B.C.

Who Were the Shang? The Shang built the first big cities. One of these was Anyang in northern China. It was China's first capital. The Shang kings ruled from there.

People in early China were divided into three major groups: the Shang kings and their families; the aristocrats, or warlords, and government officials; and the farmers. In addition, there were craftspeople and some enslaved people.

The first Shang king ruled over a small area in northern China. His armies used chariots and bronze weapons. In time, the Shang kings took over most of the Huang He valley. Later, warlords ruled portions of the area and had their own armies.

The warlords were **aristocrats.** Many aristocrats were government officials but most got their money from their land. Aristocrats passed their land—and their power—to their sons.

Most of the early Chinese were farmers. They worked on the aristocrats' farms and grew grains like millet, wheat, and rice. They also raised cattle, sheep, chickens, and pigs.

READING ESSENTIALS AND STUDY GUIDE 5-1 (continued)

Spirits and Ancestors People in Shang China worshiped many gods and goddesses. They believed that angry spirits might ruin the crops or make the army lose a battle.

They also honored their ancestors. Many believed their ancestors could bring good luck. Today, many Chinese go to temples and burn paper copies of food and clothing. These are things that their ancestors will need in the afterlife.

Telling the Future The Shang kings sought advice from gods, spirits, and ancestors. To do this, priests scratched questions on oracle bones, such as "Will I <u>recover</u> from my illness?" Then, the bones were heated until they cracked. Finally, the priests <u>interpreted</u> what the gods had "written" in the cracks for the kings.

The Chinese Language Chinese writing began as pictures. These pictures—or **pictographs**—are characters that stand for objects. Then people started putting two or more pictographs together. This is an **ideograph.** Ideographs represent ideas.

Most written languages use alphabets. An alphabet is a set of symbols that stands for sounds. The Chinese language is difficult, however. Some Chinese characters stand for sounds, but most are whole words.

Shang Artists Weavers spun silk into cloth. Artisans made vases and dishes from clay. They also made statues from ivory and jade, a rare green stone.

The Shang are best-known for their works in bronze. Bronze objects are made when molten bronze is poured into clay molds. Artisans made sculptures, vases, drinking cups, and urns.

6. What was the role of Shang warlords?

_____

_____

Academic Vocabulary
recover: to regain normal health or purpose (p. 280)

Academic Vocabulary
interpret: to explain the meaning of something (p. 280)

READING ESSENTIALS AND STUDY GUIDE 5-1 (continued)

The Zhou Dynasty (pages 281–283)

(Main Idea) Chinese rulers claimed that the Mandate of Heaven gave them the right to rule.

Shang kings treated people cruelly. There was a gap between the rich and the poor. In 1045 B.C., an aristocrat named Wu Wang rebelled. He began a new dynasty, or ruling family. It was called the Zhou.

The Zhou Government The Zhou dynasty ruled for more than 800 years. The Zhou king was the head of the government. He had to defend the kingdom against invaders.

The Zhou kings used many officials to help them run the government. These officials made up the **bureaucracy.** Like the Shang, the Zhou divided their empire into territories. Aristocrats were in charge of each territory. When an aristocrat died, his son or a relative took over.

The king's main job was to carry out religious rituals. The Chinese believed these rituals made strong <u>links</u> between people and the gods. The Zhou kings claimed that the Zhou ruled China because they had the Mandate of Heaven.

What Was the Mandate of Heaven? A **mandate** is a formal order or law. The Mandate of Heaven was a heavenly law. The Zhou said that the gods chose the king because of his talent and virtue.

The Mandate of Heaven worked in two ways. First, the people expected the king to rule by the Dao. The **Dao** means "the Way," which included keeping the gods happy. Second, it gave the people, as well as the king, important rights. For example, people could get rid of an evil ruler. Each new dynasty claimed it had the Mandate of Heaven.

Academic Vocabulary
link: to join separate things together (p. 282)

READING ESSENTIALS AND STUDY GUIDE 5-1 (continued)

New Tools and Trade During the Zhou dynasty, the Chinese improved farm tools and developed irrigation and flood-control systems. As a result, more crops could grow.

By 550 B.C., the Chinese were using iron plows. These broke up land that wooden plows could not. The Chinese could farm more land. Even more crops could grow. With more food the population grew. In the late Zhou dynasty, China had a population of about 50 million people!

Trade and manufacturing also grew. Silk, an important <u>item</u>, was traded throughout central Asia and as far away as Greece.

<table>
<tr><td>Academic Vocabulary</td></tr>
<tr><td>item: a separate part of a group (p. 283)</td></tr>
</table>

The Zhou Empire Falls Over time, the local rulers of the Zhou territories set up their own states. In 403 B.C. fighting broke out and lasted almost 200 years. This is called the "Period of the Warring States."

Aristocrats forced peasants to serve in the army. The armies fought with swords, spears, and crossbows. A crossbow uses a crank to pull a string back and shoot an arrow.

After the Chinese invented the saddle and stirrup, the cavalry was born. In 221 B.C. the ruler of Qin used his cavalry to defeat the other states. Then he set up a new dynasty.

7. What was the chief duty of Chinese kings?

_____

_____

READING ESSENTIALS AND STUDY GUIDE 5-2

Life in Ancient China *For use with pages 284–291*

Content Vocabulary

social class: includes people who share a similar position in society (page 285)

filial piety: children must respect their parents and older relatives (page 286)

Confucianism: philosophy that taught that all men, regardless of their social class, should be allowed to join the government if they can do the work (page 288)

Daoism: philosophy that promotes a peaceful society and giving up worldly desires (page 290)

Legalism: philosophy that taught that people need a "School of Law" and harsh punishments to make them do their duty (page 291)

Drawing From Experience

What do you do when your friends are fighting with each other? If you are playing a game, you can refer to the rules. If something else is causing a problem between your friends, you try another idea to solve it. Philosophers, or thinkers, have come up with many ideas for solving problems between people.

In the previous section, you learned about the Shang and Zhou dynasties. In this section, you will learn what everyday life was like during the Zhou dynasty. You will also learn about three Chinese philosophies for solving problems between people. These philosophies are Confucianism, Daoism, and Legalism.

Organizing Your Thoughts

The early Chinese thought of three ways to build peace and a good way of living. They were Confucianism, Daoism, and Legalism.

To answer the questions below, mark **C** for Confucianism, **D** for Daoism, and **L** for Legalism. Use details from the text to help you fill in the blanks.

1. Which one said that anyone could be in government if they could do the work? _____

2. Which one thought that duty was important?

_____

WH6.6 Students analyze the geographic, political, economic, religious, and social structures of the early civilizations of China.

Focuses on:
WH6.6.3, WH6.6.4

3. Which one thought that laws were important?_____

4. Which one began in the 500s B.C.? _____

5. Which one began in the 200s B.C.? _____

6. Which one thought that nature was important?

_____

7. Which one did the aristocrats like? _____

8. Which two said that you must treat other people well? _____

Life in Ancient China (pages 285–287)

Main Idea Chinese society had three main social classes: landowning aristocrats, farmers, and merchants.

A **social class** includes people who have a similar position in society. Early China had three main social classes:

- Landowning aristocrats
- Peasant farmers
- Merchants

Classes in Chinese Society China's aristocratic families owned estates. They lived in large houses. The houses had tile roofs, courtyards, and gardens. Fine furniture and silk hangings filled their rooms. Walls went around their houses to keep out bandits.

In the beginning, the estates were large. But they did not stay large. That is because each aristocrat divided his land among his sons. For example, if a man had four sons, each of them would get one-fourth of the land. As time went on, each estate got smaller and smaller.

Aristocrats did not farm their own land. Instead, farmers share-cropped it. This means that the farmers planted all of the crop but did not keep it all. In the north, the crop was a grain like wheat or millet. In the south, farmers grew rice.

READING ESSENTIALS AND STUDY GUIDE 5-2 (continued)

The farmers harvested all of the crop, too. But the farmers did not keep all of the crop. They gave most of it to the aristocrats as rent for the land. The aristocrats became very rich.

Nine out of ten Chinese were farmers. They lived in simple houses inside village walls. Most farmers owned a small piece of land where they grew food for their family. A typical family ate fish, turnips, beans, wheat and rice, and millet. The farmers paid taxes. They also had to work one month of each year on government projects like building roads. Farmers also served as soldiers.

In Chinese society, farmers ranked above merchants. The merchant social class included shopkeepers, traders, and bankers. Merchants lived in towns. They provided goods and services to the landowners.

Many merchants were very rich, but landowners and farmers still looked down on them. Chinese leaders thought that government officials should not think about money. So merchants were not allowed to have government jobs.

What Was Life Like in a Chinese Family? The family was the basic building block of Chinese society. Farming in ancient China required many workers. So people had big families. Everyone in the family—even the young children—worked in the fields. Older sons raised their own crops. They shared them with their parents. Chinese families also took care of people in need—the aged, the young, and the sick.

Chinese families practiced **filial piety.** This means that children had to respect their parents and older relatives. If the head of the family said "Do this," then everyone had to do it. The head of the family was the oldest male, usually the father. However, a son could take on this role. Then even his mother had to obey him!

Men and women had very different roles in early China. Men were respected because they grew the crops. They went to school, ran the government, and fought

READING ESSENTIALS AND STUDY GUIDE 5-2 (continued)

wars. The Chinese considered these jobs more important than the work that women did. Most women raised children and ran the house.

Chinese women could not hold government posts. However, royal women did affect government decisions. Women in the royal family often <u>convinced</u> men to do things the way that the women wanted.

Academic Vocabulary

convince: to make a person believe or agree (p. 287)

9. Why did the amount of land owned by each aristocrat decrease over time?

_____

_____

Chinese Thinkers *(pages 287–291)*

Main Idea) Three Chinese philosophies–Confucianism, Daoism, and Legalism–grew out of a need for order.

The Zhou kingdom grew weak in the 500s B.C., and violence became common. During the Period of the Warring States, whole villages of men, women, and children were beheaded. Many Chinese looked for a way to restore peace and order.

Chinese thinkers developed three major ideas about making a peaceful society. These theories are Confucianism, Daoism, and Legalism.

Who Was Confucius? Confucius was ancient China's first great thinker and teacher. Confucius wanted to end the problems in China. He tried to bring peace to society.

Confucius believed that people needed a sense of duty. Duty meant that people should not think of themselves first. He said that people must put the needs of family and community first.

Confucius said that each person owed a duty to another person. Parents owed their children love. Children owed their parents honor. Husbands owed their wives support, wives owed their husbands obedience.

Most of all, the rulers had to set good examples. If a king ruled well, his subjects would respect him. Society would be strong and good.

Confucius believed that society would be fine if each person did his or her duty. He also urged people to be good and to seek knowledge. He said:

> "There are those who act without knowing; I will have none of this. To hear a lot, choose the good, and follow it, to see a lot and learn to recognize it: this is next to knowledge."
> —Confucius, *Analects*

Confucius asked people to treat each other well. He told people to "measure the feelings of others by one's own," for "within the four seas all men are brothers." This means that everyone has the same basic feelings and needs. We should think about what we do to others. If we would not like it being done to us, then we should not do it to anyone else. Confucius thought that there would be peace if people treated each other this way.

Confucius traveled through China teaching his ideas. These ideas became **Confucianism.** Confucius said that all men—not just aristocrats—should be part of the government. At that time, the government officials were all aristocrats. They did not like his ideas!

Other people liked his ideas, though. Over time, Confucius won many followers. They honored him as a great teacher. They wrote down his sayings and carried his message. Confucius died in 479 B.C., but his sayings are still taught today.

What Is Daoism? **Daoism** is another Chinese philosophy that <u>promotes</u> a peaceful society. Daoism is also called Taoism. It is based on the Dao, or the "force that guides all

Academic Vocabulary
promote: to help grow or develop (p. 290)

things." Tradition says that Laozi, or the Old Master, first taught Daoism. No one knows if Laozi was a real person, but tradition says that he lived around the same time as Confucius. Daoism became popular between 500 B.C. and 300 B.C.

The ideas of Daoism are written in *Dao De Jing*. Daoists believed that people should stop wanting worldly things like money or fame. Instead, people should follow nature and the Dao. To show how to follow the Dao, Daoists used examples from nature:

> "Higher good is like water: the good in water bene-
> fits all, and does so without contention. It rests
> where people dislike to be, so it is close to the Way.
> Where it dwells becomes good ground; profound is
> the good in its heart, Benevolent the good it
> bestows."
> —Laozi, *Tao Te Ching*

In some ways, Daoism is the opposite of Confucianism. Confucius taught that people should try to improve the world. Daoism tells people to give up their concerns about the world. It says they should seek inner peace. They should live in harmony with nature. Many Chinese followed both Confucianism and Daoism.

What Is Legalism? A third group of thinkers thought that strong laws were the only thing that would bring peace. People called their thinking **Legalism.** This means the "School of Law."

A scholar named Hanfeizi developed Legalism during the 200s B.C. Confucius and Laozi thought that people were basically good. Hanfeizi did not. Hanfeizi taught that humans were naturally evil. He thought that they needed laws and punishments to make them do their duty. His followers believed that only a strong ruler could keep peace.

READING ESSENTIALS AND STUDY GUIDE 5-2 (continued)

Many aristocrats liked Legalism. One reason was that Legalism said that rulers did not have to be good to the lower classes. Legalism let the aristocrats pass laws to control the farmers.

10. Why did Hanfeizi believe that people needed laws and punishments?

_____

_____

READING ESSENTIALS AND STUDY GUIDE 5-3

The Qin and Han Dynasties *For use with pages 294–303*

Content Vocabulary

acupuncture: sticking thin needles into specific points on a patient's body to relieve pain (page 300)

Drawing From Experience

Have you ever eaten a peanut butter sandwich? How about an orange from Florida or an apple from Washington? We get our food, clothes, and other things from all around the United States and the world. As we get goods from other places, we also learn about different ideas. People have always shared ideas as they traded goods.

In the previous section, you learned about China's early dynasties. In this section, you will learn about the Qin and Han dynasties. You will also learn about trade on the "Silk Road," and about how Buddhism spread into China.

WH6.6 Students analyze the geographic, political, economic, religious, and social structures of the early civilizations of China.

Focuses on:

WH6.6.5, WH6.6.6, WH6.6.7, WH6.6.8

Organizing Your Thoughts

Many things were invented during the Han dynasty. Use details from the text to help you fill in the blanks.

Medicine	1.
Mining and ironwork	2.
Government	3.
Ships	4.
Mills	5.

READING ESSENTIALS AND STUDY GUIDE 5-3 (continued)

Emperor Qin Shihuangdi (pages 295–296)

Main Idea Qin Shihuangdi used harsh methods to unify and defend China.

From about 400 B.C. to 200 B.C., the rulers of local states fought one another. Eventually, Qin took over its neighboring states. In 221 B.C., the ruler declared himself Qin Shihuangdi which means "the First Qin Emperor." The Qin ruler made changes in China's government that would last for 2,000 years.

A Powerful Ruler Qin used the ideas of Legalism. Anyone who did not agree with him was punished. Many people were killed. Books that did not agree with him were publicly burned.

Qin made the central government stronger. He appointed government officials called censors. Censors made sure that other government officials did their jobs.

Second in power to the central government were provinces and counties. In the provinces, the officials used to pass their posts on to sons or relatives. Qin changed that. He now filled those jobs with his friends and other people loyal to him.

Qin created one <u>currency</u>, or type of money. Everyone in the empire used that money. He also built roads and a huge canal. The canal connected the Chang Jiang in central China to the city of Guangzhou in southern China. He used the canal to ship supplies to his armies all over China.

The Great Wall The Gobi is located at China's northern border. Nomads lived in the Gobi. Nomads are people who move from place to place with herds of animals. The Chinese called the nomads the Xiongnu. The Xiongnu were masters at fighting on horseback. They often attacked Chinese farms and villages. Several Chinese rulers in the north built walls to keep out the Xiongnu.

Qin thought that walls were a good idea. He forced farmers to connect and strengthen the walls with stone, sand, and trash. The result was the Great Wall of China! However, Qin did not build the wall that we know today. That was built 1,500 years later.

Academic Vocabulary
currency: a type of money (p. 296)

READING ESSENTIALS AND STUDY GUIDE 5-3 (continued)

Why did People Rebel? Many Chinese thought Qin was a cruel leader. Aristocrats were angry because he reduced their power. Scholars hated him for burning their writings. Farmers hated him for making them build roads and the Great Wall. Qin died in 210 B.C. Four years later, the people overthrew his dynasty. Civil war followed. Soon there was a new dynasty.

> **Academic Vocabulary**
>
> **civil:** an issue or problem between citizens of the same country or nation (p. 296)

6. Why did no one rebel against Qin?

_____

_____

The Han Dynasty *(pages 298–300)*

Main Idea Developments during the Han dynasty improved life for all Chinese.

> **Academic Vocabulary**
>
> **found:** to start or establish (p. 298)

In 202 B.C. Liu Bang founded the Han dynasty. Born a peasant, he became a military leader.

Liu Bang called himself Han Gaozu, which means "Exalted Emperor of Han." Han Gaozu threw out the harsh policies of the Qin dynasty. But he still used censors to watch the other officials. He also kept the empire divided into provinces and counties.

What Was the Civil Service? Han Wudi was one of the greatest Han leaders. Han Wudi means "Martial Emperor of Han." He ruled from 141 B.C. to 87 B.C.

Wudi gave tests to the people looking for jobs. The people with the highest scores got the jobs. In time, Wudi's tests became the civil service examinations. The Chinese chose their government officials this way for 2,000 years. The system favored the rich. Only they could educate their sons for the exams.

Students prepared for these tests for years. They studied law, history, and the teachings of Confucius. After many years of schooling, the students took the exams. Only one in five passed. People who failed the exams taught or worked for government officials.

READING ESSENTIALS AND STUDY GUIDE 5-3 (continued)

The Chinese Empire Grows The rulers needed a large bureaucracy to help them keep order. That was hard because the empire grew from 20 million people to more than 60 million people!

Some changes occurred in how land was divided. Farmers used to divide their land among their sons. After many years, the average farm was too small to grow crops. So many farmers sold their land to an aristocrat. The farmers became tenant farmers, or people who work on land owned by someone else. They paid rent for the land in crops. Soon the aristocrats owned thousands of acres.

China kept growing. Han armies added lands to the south and west. They also drove back the Xiongnu, or the nomads to the north. The Han dynasty also made the country more <u>secure</u>. After Wudi's death, the Chinese lived in peace for almost 150 years.

Academic Vocabulary
secure: to provide safety (p. 299)

An Era of Inventions New inventions during the Han dynasty helped Chinese workers produce more goods. Waterwheels, iron drill bits, steel, and paper were all invented.

Chinese medicine improved, too. Doctors discovered that certain foods prevented disease. They used herbs to cure illnesses. They also stuck thin needles into people to get rid of pain. This treatment is known as **acupuncture.**

The Chinese invented the rudder to steer ships and a new way to move the sails of ships. These changes allowed ships to sail into the wind for the first time. Now Chinese merchant ships could travel to the islands of Southeast Asia and into the Indian Ocean. As a result, China established trade in India and the Mediterranean Sea.

7. How did China's empire increase in size during the Han dynasty?

_____

_____

READING ESSENTIALS AND STUDY GUIDE 5-3 (continued)

The Silk Road (pages 300–302)

Main Idea The Silk Road carried Chinese goods as far as Greece and Rome.

Chinese merchants shipped expensive things like silk to other countries. Some of it went by ship. However, most went overland on the Silk Road.

What Was the Silk Road? Merchants began using the Silk Road after Han Wudi sent out a general to explore areas west of China. The general's name was Zhang Qian. Thirteen years later, Zhang returned to China. He had found a western kingdom where there were large, strong horses. This was good news to Emperor Wudi. His troops were mostly made up of an army who went on foot. His enemy's troops were cavalry—they rode horses. The emperor encouraged trade in order to get those horses and defeat the enemy. As a result, the Silk Road was developed. It was actually not one road, but a network of trade routes. It stretched 4,000 miles, from western China to southwest Asia.

Merchants used camels to carry their goods across deserts and mountains to central Asia. From there, Arabs carried them to the Mediterranean Sea.

The trip over the Silk Road was difficult, dangerous and expensive. Merchants carried only silk, spices, tea, and porcelain. People paid a lot for these things, so the merchants made big profits. This made the trip over the Silk Road worthwhile. These profits also helped pay the taxes along the Silk Road.

The Impact of the Silk Road General Zhang hadn't just seen horses in the west. He had also seen people "who cut their hair short, wear embroidered clothes, and ride in very small chariots." What he was describing was the Roman Empire in the west.

The trade that developed along the Silk Road brought China into contact with many other civilizations. The Chinese were linked to people in Southeast Asia, southern India, and Egypt.

READING ESSENTIALS AND STUDY GUIDE 5-3 (continued)

As the years passed, many items were traded besides silk. Fruit, vegetables, flowers, grains and other products made their way back and forth across the Silk Road. Eventually, Chinese technological advances, such as paper, journeyed to other countries along the Silk Road.

8. Why were only expensive goods carried on the Silk Road?

_____

_____

Major Changes in China *(page 303)*

Main Idea) Unrest in China helped Buddhism to spread.

Merchants and teachers from India brought Buddhism to China during the A.D. 100s. Many Chinese began to believe in Buddhism partially because of the fall of the Han dynasty.

The Han emperors after Wudi were weak and foolish. People did not respect the rulers. The central government lost power because its rulers could not keep control. The aristocrats began stealing land from farmers. And the farmers got upset because the central government was not protecting them. They rebelled.

There were wars and plots against the emperor, too. This ended the Han dynasty. A rebel army attacked the capital of Luoyang in A.D. 190. By A.D. 220, China was in a civil war. To make things worse, the nomads invaded the country.

Many Chinese felt unsafe. Buddhist ideas helped people cope with their stress and fear. Followers of Confucius became Buddhists, too. So did many Daoists. By the A.D. 400s, Buddhism was popular in China.

9. What groups in China were the first to adopt Buddhism?

_____

_____

READING ESSENTIALS AND STUDY GUIDE 6-1

The First Americans *For use with pages 312–316*

Content Vocabulary

glacier: huge sheet of ice (page 313)

Drawing from Experience

Have you ever planted a garden or tried to grow something? What happened to your plants? What would your life be like if people had never learned to farm?

In this section, you will learn about the first people to come to the Americas. You'll also learn about how farming began.

WH7.7 Students compare and contrast the geographic, political, economic, religious, and social structures of the Meso-American and Andean civilizations.

Focuses on:

WH7.7.1

Organizing Your Thoughts

Use the time line to help you take notes on the first people in the Americas. List dates for the events listed below.

1. Teotihuacán reaches its height
2. Mayan civilization begins
3. Moche rule begins
4. Olmec build an empire
5. Moche rule ends

1200 B.C. _____ A.D. 700

READING ESSENTIALS AND STUDY GUIDE 6-1 (continued)

Farming in Mesoamerica *(pages 313–314)*

Main Idea People came to the Americas during the Ice Age, and about 10,000 years ago, farming began in Mesoamerica.

How did people first come to America? A long time ago, America was connected by land to the rest of the world. During the Ice Age, the earth became very cold. Scientists have studied the earth's surface during the Ice Age. They think that much of the earth's water froze into huge sheets of ice, or **glaciers.**

As the ice froze, the seas fell. Dry land was <u>exposed</u> between Asia and Alaska. Scientists call this land bridge Beringia. It is named after Vitus Bering, a European explorer. They think that people in Asia followed animals across the land bridge into the Americas. Scientists tested the age of bones and tools in very old campsites. Based on these tests, scientists <u>estimate</u> that the first people came between 15,000 and 40,000 years ago.

The Ice Age ended about 10,000 years ago. The glaciers melted and the water went back into the seas. The land bridge to America was covered by water.

Hunting and Gathering Hunters in the Americas were always moving and looking for food. They fished and gathered nuts, fruits, or roots. They also hunted huge animals such as the woolly mammoth, antelope, caribou, and bison.

A woolly mammoth could weigh as much as 9 tons. It took several hunters to kill it. They got meat, hides for clothing, and bones for tools from these big animals.

With the end of the Ice Age, some animals disappeared from the earth. But the warm weather was good for early Americans.

The Agricultural Revolution in America The first Americans were hunter-gatherers. But the end of the Ice Age brought warmer weather, and people learned something new. They learned that they could plant seeds that would grow into crops for food.

Academic Vocabulary
expose: to lay open (p. 313)

Academic Vocabulary
estimate: a guess based on evidence (p. 313)

READING ESSENTIALS AND STUDY GUIDE 6-1 (continued)

Farming began 9,000 to 10,000 years ago in Meso-america. *Meso* comes from the Greek word for "middle." This area includes lands from the Valley of Mexico to Costa Rica in Central America.

The land in this area was good for farming. A lot of the area had rich soil from volcanoes. It also had a warm climate. Rain in the spring helped seeds grow. Dryer weather in the summer helped the crops get ripe. More rain in the fall made the soil wet for next year's crops.

The first American crops included pumpkins, peppers, squash, gourds, and beans. Corn grew as a wild grass with only one, one-inch cob. After hundreds of years, the early Americans learned how to cross corn with other grasses to get bigger cobs. They also learned how to grow more cobs on each plant. This made corn, also called maize, the most important food in the Americas.

6. When did the first people come to the Americas?

_____

_____

Early American Civilizations *(pages 315–316)*

Main Idea The first civilizations in America were based on farming and trade.

When Mesoamericans started growing crops, they could stop moving around looking for food. Their societies changed. The first civilization appeared around 1500 B.C.

Who Were the Olmec? Around 1200 B.C., people called the Olmec built a trading empire. It lasted about 800 years. They lived near today's city of Vera Cruz, Mexico.

The Olmec had good land for farming. But they did not have other things they needed. They traded salt and beans to get jade for jewelry. They traded for obsidian, or volcanic glass, to make sharp knives. They used a shiny volcanic stone to make polished mirrors. And they used basalt for carving big stone heads.

READING ESSENTIALS AND STUDY GUIDE 6-1 (continued)

The Olmec used the area's many rivers for trade, but in time the inland peoples took control of the trade. One of these groups built the first planned city in the Americas. It was known as Teotihuacán, or "Place of the Gods." The city was at its most powerful around A.D. 400. Between 120,000 and 200,000 people lived there.

Who Were the Maya? As Teotihuacán became more powerful, a people called the Maya built another civilization. They lived in the wet rain forests of the Yucatán Peninsula. They also traded. Their location made it easy for them to reach as far as southern Mexico and Central America. Mayan traders in canoes paddled along the coast. They may have gone as far north as the present-day United States.

The Moche Other civilizations grew south of Mesoamerica. The Moche people lived in the dry desert along the coast of South America. Today, this is called Peru.

The Moche ruled from about A.D. 100 to A.D. 700. They dug canals to bring water from the Andes mountain ranges. Because of this water, they could grow crops in the desert.

The Moche grew lots of food. They ate corn, squash, beans, and peanuts. They also hunted llamas and guinea pigs. They fished in the Pacific Ocean.

Because they did not have to worry about food, the Moche could do other things. They built big pyramids, and they traded with people as far away as the Amazon River valley. Their goods included pottery, cloth, and jewelry.

The Moche did many things. But they never grew far beyond their homeland. A people called the Inca eventually replaced them.

7. How did the ability to farm change life in these ancient civilizations?

_____

_____

READING ESSENTIALS AND STUDY GUIDE 6-2

The Mayan People *For use with pages 317–321*

Content Vocabulary

sinkhole: area in the ground where the earth has fallen in (page 318)

alliance: agreement of people or states to work together (page 320)

Drawing From Experience

Have you ever lived in or visited a different part of your country? Was it warmer? Colder? How did these differences affect the lives of people living there?

The last section described the first civilizations in the Americas. This section discusses Mayan culture.

Organizing Your Thoughts

Use the diagram to help you take notes. Fill in the diagram to help you learn about the achievements of the Maya.

WH7.7 Students compare and contrast the geographic, political, economic, religious, and social structures of the Meso-American and Andean civilizations.

Focuses on:

WH7.7.1, WH7.7.2, WH7.7.4, WH7.7.5

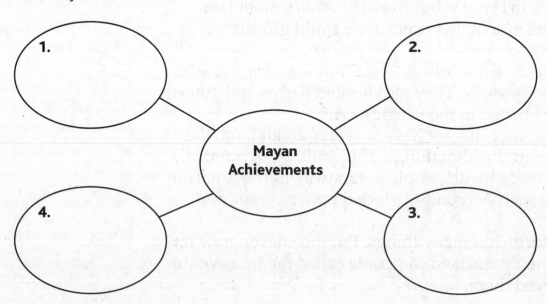

1.

2.

Mayan Achievements

4.

3.

READING ESSENTIALS AND STUDY GUIDE 6-2 (continued)

The Mayan People (pages 318–319)

Main Idea The Maya created a civilization of city-states and thrived in Mesoamerica's rain forest.

In A.D. 1839, John Lloyd Stevens and Frederick Catherwood found the ruins of an ancient city. Stevens was an American lawyer. Catherwood was an English artist. As they cut their way through the Yucatán rain forest, they made a great discovery.

Stevens and Catherwood learned that the people who built the city were called the Maya. These people were related to the millions of Maya who still live today in Mexico, Guatemala, Honduras, El Salvador, and Belize.

It looked at first like the Maya lived in one of the worst spots on Earth. They picked the Petén in present-day Guatemala. *Petén* is the Mayan word for "flat region." The forests there nearly blocked out the sun.

The Maya saw the good things about their land. Swamps and **sinkholes** gave them <u>access</u> to a steady source of water. Sinkholes are areas where the earth has fallen. These holes gave the Maya a system of underground rivers and streams. They served as Mayan wells.

The Maya had water. But without an organized culture, they could not have built cities and fields in this land. Many people had to work together. This meant they needed an organized government.

The Maya set up city-states. Rulers in each city-state gave the leadership and military force needed for building projects. Leadership was passed from one king to the next. The city-states often fought with each other.

Academic Vocabulary
access: to gain use of or have available (p. 318)

5. What was the main advantage of the Maya location?

_____

_____

READING ESSENTIALS AND STUDY GUIDE 6-2 (continued)

Mayan Culture *(pages 320–321)*

Main Idea The Maya developed a society of city-states and a culture based on their religion.

Mayan rulers said they came from the sun. They said they had the right to rule as god-kings. They expected every person to serve them. They also expected people to put up big buildings or statues to honor them.

Life in Mayan Cities Mayan rulers told the people how to make the gods happy. One way was by killing people. In battle, the Maya wanted to take people more than they wanted to take land. During times when they had no rain, Mayan priests killed the captives. The deaths were an offering to Chac, the god of rain and sunlight.

The Maya believed that the gods controlled all of life on Earth. For this reason, religion was at the center of Mayan life. Every city had a huge pyramid with a temple at the top. Priests set up a class system. In this system, everyone had a place.

Royal Mayan women often married into royal families in faraway city-states. This helped with trade. It also helped form **alliances.** Alliances are agreements to work together.

Women played a big role in the city-states. In the city-state of Calakmul, women sometimes served as powerful queens.

Mayan Science and Writing Both queens and kings asked Mayan priests for help. The priests thought that the gods showed their plans through the sun, moon, and stars. They studied the sky closely.

The sky also showed the Maya when to plant their crops. By watching the sky, the priests made a 365-day calendar to track the stars and planets. They used it to predict eclipses and to plan religious festivals, plantings, and harvests. To track time, the Maya developed a system of math.

Academic Vocabulary
predict: to guess about what will happen in the future (p. 321)

READING ESSENTIALS AND STUDY GUIDE 6-2 (continued)

The Maya also invented a written language. They used it to write numbers and dates. Like the Egyptians, the Maya used a system of symbols. Symbols stood for words, sounds, or ideas. But only nobles could read them. After the end of the Mayan civilization, no one could read them at all. But today people have started to understand the stories told by the symbols.

What Happened to the Maya? Mayan cities were at their best in the A.D. 500s. Over the next 300 years, the Mayan city-states started to weaken. No one knows why. Some believe that there was not enough food for so many people. Others believe they had a long period without rain. Still others say that the poor people turned against their rich rulers. Whatever the reason, the Maya were gone by the A.D. 900s.

6. Who was Chac?

_____

_____

READING ESSENTIALS AND STUDY GUIDE 7-1

The Early Greeks   *For use with pages 336–343*

Content Vocabulary

peninsula: a body of land with water on three sides (page 337)

polis: a Greek city-state (page 341)

agora: an open area used for a market and meeting place (page 341)

colony: settlement in a new territory that stays closely linked to its homeland (page 343)

Drawing From Experience

What if generations of your family lived along the coast? Chances are good that your father was a fisher-man—or your grandfather fixed boats for a living.

Geography would influence their way of life.

In this section, you will learn how geography determined the rise and spread of the early Greek kingdoms.

WH6.4 Students analyze the geographic, political, economic, religious, and social structures of the early civilizations of Ancient Greece.

Focuses on:
WH6.4.1, WH6.4.2

Organizing Your Thoughts

Use the following 4 W's and an H chart to track how geography influenced the early Minoans and Mycenaeans. Use details from the text to help you fill in each blank.

Early Greeks	Minoans	Mycenaeans
WHO were they?	1.	6.
WHERE did they live?	2.	7.
WHAT geographical features shaped their land?	3.	8.
HOW did geography influence them?	4.	9.
WHY did their kingdom fall?	5.	10.

READING ESSENTIALS AND STUDY GUIDE 7-1 (continued)

The Geography of Greece (page 337)

Main Idea The geography of Greece influenced where people settled and what they did.

Greece is a **peninsula**—land with water on three sides. The Ionian Sea is in the west. The Aegean Sea is in the east. The Mediterranean Sea is in the south. In these waters are hundreds of islands. The islands are covered with mountain ridges, hills, and forests. This geography helped shape Greek history.

The nearby sea led many ancient Greeks to fish or build boats. Others sailed across the sea to trade goods with other lands. The nearby mountains and rocky soil made farming a challenge. However, warm, mild weather made it possible to grow wheat, barley, olives, and grapes.

Greece's seas and mountains also shaped its society. They divided the land. Early Greek communities became isolated from each other. But this made them stronger. They became independent.

11. Name two ways that the sea influenced early Greeks and their societies.

_____

_____

The Minoans (page 338)

Main Idea The Minoans earned their living by building ships and trading.

The island of Crete lies southeast of the Greek mainland. In 1900, a British archaeologist named Arthur Evans went there. In Knossos, he uncovered the ruins of a Minoan palace. The Minoans had developed the first civilization in the <u>region</u>. This palace had once been the center of Minoan life. Its ruins had private rooms for the royal family, bathrooms, storerooms, and workshops.

Academic Vocabulary

region: broad geographical area (p. 338)

The Minoans used the oak and cedar trees from the forests of Crete. They built wooden ships that could sail as far as Egypt and Syria.

Minoan traders left port with pottery and stone vases. They returned with ivory and metals. Their island location worked well. They could control trade on the Mediterranean Sea.

By 2000 B.C., Minoan society was thriving. But by 1450 B.C., it had collapsed. Historians disagree about what caused the downfall. Some think undersea earthquakes crushed Minoan cities under giant waves. Others believe invaders from the mainland caused the destruction.

12. What helped the Minoans become great traders?

_____

_____

The First Greek Kingdoms (pages 339–340)

Main Idea Mycenaeans built the first Greek kingdoms and spread their power across the Mediterranean region.

The Mycenaeans first came from central Asia. In 1900 B.C., they invaded the Greek mainland and conquered its people.

What Were Mycenaean Kingdoms Like? In the late 1800s B.C., the ruins of a walled palace were discovered in Mycenae. Long ago, a palace stood at the center of each Mycenaean kingdom. Built on a hill, each palace lay near farms and estates. These lands belonged to the nobles. Slaves and farmers lived there. The palace was home to artisans, government officials, and civic life.

Power From Trade and War Minoan traders soon visited Mycenae from Crete. The Mycenaeans learned much about Minoan <u>culture</u>. They learned bronze-working, ship-building, navigation, and religion. Around 1400 B.C., they replaced the Minoans as the major power on the

Academic Vocabulary
culture: particular form or style of a society (p. 339)

READING ESSENTIALS AND STUDY GUIDE 7-1 (continued)

Mediterranean. However, 300 years later, earthquakes and in-fighting destroyed their civilization.

What Was the Dark Age? Between 1100 B.C. and 750 B.C. was the Dark Age. Farmers grew only enough to feed their families, so there was no surplus food. Poverty set in. <u>Overseas</u> trade slowed down. Craft skills died out. Teachers stopped teaching. And Greeks forgot their written language.

During the Dark Age, thousands of Greeks moved to islands in the Aegean Sea. Still others moved to Asia Minor, to what is now Turkey. This expanded Greek culture.

Meanwhile, people known as Dorians invaded Greece. They settled on the Peloponnesus peninsula. The Dorians brought iron weapons. Greeks had used bronze, but iron was stronger and cheaper. The Dorians gave Greece more advanced technology.

Over time, Greek farmers grew more food. Traders came into contact with new ways of writing. The idea for a Greek alphabet came from the Phoenicians to the east. The new, simpler alphabet helped the Greeks revive reading, writing, and storytelling.

> **Academic Vocabulary**
>
> **overseas:** across the sea or ocean (p. 340)

13. Name two positive changes that occurred during Greece's Dark Age.

_____

_____

The Polis (pages 341–342)

Main Idea The idea of citizenship developed in Greek city-states.

By the end of the Dark Age, Greek society had changed. Instead of kingdoms, there were city-states. Each city-state, or **polis,** was made up of a town and its nearby area. Each polis had an acropolis, or main gathering place. The fortified acropolis sat on a hill. It

READING ESSENTIALS AND STUDY GUIDE 7-1 (continued)

could also be a religious center. Each polis also had an **agora.** This open area below the acropolis was a market and a meeting place.

What Was Greek Citizenship? The Greeks were the first to develop the idea of citizenship. Each Greek city-state was run by its citizens or members of a political <u>community</u> who treated each other as equals and who had rights and responsibilities.

In ancient Greece, only free, native-born men who owned land could be citizens. Some city-states, such as Athens, dropped the land-owning requirement. Still, slaves and foreign-born residents were excluded. Women and children could qualify for citizenship. However, they had no citizens' rights. Citizens could choose officials and pass laws, vote, hold office, own property, and defend themselves in court.

Citizens as Soldiers Greek citizenship also included certain duties. Each citizen had to serve in government. They also had to fight for their polis as citizen-soldiers. Since the rise of city-states, wars were no longer waged by nobles riding horses and chariots. By 700 B.C., each polis depended on an army of citizen-soldiers called hoplites.

Hoplites fought on foot. Each soldier had a shield, a short sword, and a spear. They went into battle in rows. They used their shields as one long protective wall.

Hoplites made good soldiers because they were citizens. They took pride in fighting for their own city-states. However, this "hometown" loyalty caused division and distrust among Greeks as a whole.

Academic Vocabulary
community: a group of people with common interests and shared rights (p. 341)

14. How was citizenship in ancient Greece different from citizenship as we know it today?

_____

_____

READING ESSENTIALS AND STUDY GUIDE 7-1 (continued)

A Move to Colonize (page 343)

Main Idea Colonies and trade spread Greek culture and spurred industry.

Greece's recovery from its Dark Age led to three important developments:

• **Colonization** The population quickly began to outgrow Greek cities. People started Greek **colonies.** A colony is a settlement in a new area. Between 750 B.C. and 550 B.C., Greek colonies spread to Italy, France, Spain, North Africa, and western Asia. These colonies produced grain and other foods that could be exported to city-states with growing populations.

• **Coins** As trade grew, the Greeks began to make, or "mint," coins. Merchants had traded with goods. Now, they "traded" for money. This gave trade a strong boost.

• **Specialization** As demand for goods quickly grew, people in different areas specialized in making certain products. For example, areas rich in clay specialized in making pottery.

15. How did minting coins help the growth of Greek civilization?

_____

_____

READING ESSENTIALS AND STUDY GUIDE 7-2

Sparta and Athens *For use with pages 344–350*

Content Vocabulary

tyrant: someone who takes power by force and rules with authority (page 345)

oligarchy: rule by the few (page 346)

democracy: citizen-run government (page 346)

helot: workers captured and enslaved by the Spartans (page 346)

Drawing From Experience

Most people experience power struggles in their daily lives. Sometimes, a bully uses force to get his way. Or a group of popular friends can set trends by excluding others. Often, different kinds of people can band together when they become unhappy with a "leader."

In the previous section, you learned about the geography of Greece. In this section, you will learn how two Greek city-states found different methods of running—and changing—their governments.

WH6.4 Students analyze the geographic, political, economic, religious, and social structures of the early civilizations of Ancient Greece.

Focuses on:

WH6.4.2, WH6.4.6

Organizing Your Thoughts

Use the following chart to note similarities and differences between Athens and Sparta. Use details from the text to help you fill in each category.

	Sparta	Athens
System of government	1.	6.
Government details	2.	7.
Expansion method	3.	8.
Boy's life	4.	9.
Girl's life	5.	10.

READING ESSENTIALS AND STUDY GUIDE 7-2 (continued)

Tyranny in the City-States *(pages 345–346)*

Main Idea Tyrants were able to seize power from the nobles with the support of Greek farmers, merchants, and artisans.

Small farmers often needed money to live on until they could harvest and sell their crops. They borrowed this money from the nobles. If the farmers could not pay their debts on time, the nobles took their land. Many farmers lost their land. They had to work directly for the nobles or become city laborers. Desperate farmers sometimes sold themselves into slavery.

By 650 B.C., small farmers joined merchants and artisans in demanding change. Merchants and artisans had become wealthy through trade. But they did not own land. Therefore, they could not become citizens. They had no voice in running the polis.

This unrest led to the rise of tyrants. A **tyrant** is someone who takes power by force and rules with total authority. Today we think of tyrants as being harsh. Early Greek tyrants were wise and fair. They built new marketplaces, temples, and walls. Still, most Greeks wanted to be citizens.

By 500 B.C., most city-states had replaced the tyrants. Two new types of government arose. The first was **oligarchy,** in which a few people hold power. The second was **democracy,** which is run by citizens. Sparta had an oligarchy. Athens had a democracy. They were both powerful Greek city-states.

11. Who joined with farmers in demanding change?

_____

_____

Sparta (pages 346–347)

Main Idea The Spartans focused on military skills to control the people they conquered.

Like other city-states, Sparta needed more land as it grew. Unlike other city-states, Sparta did not set up colonies. Instead, Spartans conquered and enslaved their neighbors. They called their slaves **helots.**

Why Was the Military So Important? Spartans worried that the helots might rebel. So the government set up strict military training.

At age seven, boys went to live in army barracks. They were toughened with harsh treatment. At age 20, Spartan men entered the army and stayed for ten years. Only then, could they return home. But they stayed in the army until age 60. All were expected to win or die on the battlefield, but never to surrender.

Girls kept fit by running, wrestling, and throwing long, thin spears called javelins. Wives stayed home while their husbands lived in the barracks. As a result, Spartan women were freer than other Greek women. They could own property and go where they pleased.

What Was Sparta's Government Like? Under the Spartan oligarchy, two kings headed a council of elders. The council's function was to present laws to an assembly. It included 28 citizens over age 60. All Spartan men over age 30 belonged to an assembly. They voted on council law. They also chose five people to be ephors. An ephor <u>enforced</u> laws and managed tax collection.

The government adopted several policies to keep people from questioning their system, including:

- limiting foreign visitors
- banning travel abroad
- discouraging the study of literature and the arts

The Spartans successfully controlled the helots for almost 250 years. But their focus on the military came at a price. They fell behind other Greeks in trade. Their

> **Academic Vocabulary**
>
> **enforce:** to make sure laws are carried out correctly (p. 347)

READING ESSENTIALS AND STUDY GUIDE 7-2 (continued)

knowledge of science and other subjects was poor. Still, their soldiers would play a key role in defending Greece.

12. How did ordinary citizens play a role in the Spartan oligarchy?

_____

_____

Athens (pages 348–350)

Main Idea Unlike Spartans, Athenians were more interested in building a democracy than building a military force.

What Was Life in Athens Like? Athens was at least a two-day trip from Sparta. The governments of the two city-states were very different.

In Athens, citizens raised their children under a different set of values. In schools, one teacher taught reading, writing, and math. Another teacher led sports activities. A third teacher focused on music. This included singing and playing a stringed instrument called a lyre. As you can tell, Athenians believed in creating well-rounded citizens—in both body and mind.

At age 18, boys finished school and became citizens. Girls stayed at home. There, mothers taught them household duties like spinning and weaving. Some wealthy families taught their daughters to read, write, and play the lyre.

A Budding Democracy During the 600s B.C., Athens was ruled by landowning nobles. Then, farmers began to rebel. They demanded an end to all debts, and land for the poor. The nobles knew they were in trouble. So in 594 B.C., they called upon a noble named Solon. This man was trusted by both sides.

Solon acted swiftly. First, he cancelled all debts. He also freed farmers who were forced to become slaves. Then he allowed all male citizens to <u>participate</u> in the

Academic Vocabulary

participate: take part in an activity or gathering (p. 349)

assembly and law courts. Solon's reforms were popular among common people. But they did not address one key issue: Solon refused to give away wealthy nobles' land.

After Solon, 30 years of turmoil gripped Athens. Finally, a tyrant named Peisistratus seized power in 560 B.C. He did several things to win support of the poor. He divided large estates among landless farmers. He also loaned money to the poor. And he gave them jobs building temples and other public works.

The next important leader was Cleisthenes. When he took power in 508 B.C., he reorganized the assembly to play a central role. Now, members had new powers. They could participate in open debate, hear court cases, and appoint army generals. Cleisthenes also created a new 500-citizen assembly to conduct daily business. This council proposed laws, dealt with foreign countries, and oversaw the treasury. The new council was an important development for democracy. Athenians chose its members by lottery each year. They believed this system was fairer because an election might favor the rich.

Cleisthenes' reforms did not bring women, foreign-born men, and slaves into the political process. Still, he is credited with bringing democracy to Athens.

13. Name one way that Cleisthenes made the government of Athens more democratic.

_____

_____

Reading Essentials and Study Guide 7-3

Persia Attacks the Greeks *For use with pages 351–357*

Content Vocabulary

satrapies: the 20 states of the Persian Empire (page 353)

satrap: official ruler of a Persian state (page 353)

Zoroastrianism: Persian religion founded on principle of one god (page 353)

Drawing From Experience

Three of you are working on a class project. Two of you argue about what to do. The third student starts bullying you to do what he or she wants. Would you and your classmate band together to stop the bully?

In the previous section, you learned about government in Greece. In this section, you will learn how Greek city-states put aside their differences to resist the Persian Empire.

WH6.4 Students analyze the geographic, political, economic, religious, and social structures of the early civilizations of Ancient Greece.

Focuses on:

WH6.4.5, WH6.4.6

Organizing Your Thoughts

Use the following time line to track the major events that occurred between 539 B.C. and 334 B.C. Use details from the text to help you.

Date	539 B.C.	521 B.C.	499 B.C.	490 B.C.	480 B.C.	479 B.C.	334 B.C.
Events	1.	2.	3.	4.	5.	6.	7.

The Persian Empire *(pages 352–353)*

Main Idea The Persian Empire united a wide area under a single government.

Long ago, the people of Persia lived in what is known today as southwestern Iran. For a time, Persians were warriors and nomads, or wanderers, who herded cattle. In 559 B.C., Cyrus the Great united Persians into a powerful

READING ESSENTIALS AND STUDY GUIDE 7-3 (continued)

kingdom. Then he built his kingdom into the largest empire in the world.

The Rise of the Persian Empire Persia's conquests began in 539 B.C. First, Cyrus's armies captured Babylon. Then, they took over northern Mesopotamia. On and on the armies marched, sweeping into Asia Minor, Syria, Canaan, and the Phoenician cities. Cyrus treated his new subjects well. This helped hold his growing empire together.

The rule of Cyrus the Great ended in 530 B.C. The leaders who followed continued to add new territory—Egypt, western India, and Thrace, a region northeast of Greece. Now, the empire was about the size of the continental United States.

Such a large empire presented a problem: How could Persia connect all its holdings? Leaders conquered this challenge by building miles and miles of roads. The largest was the Royal Road, which stretched from Asia Minor to the Persian capital of Susa. Along the roadside were stations that supplied travelers with food, shelter, and fresh horses.

What Was Persian Government Like? The empire's growth meant more difficulties. Leaders found government hard to manage. When Darius came to the throne in 521 B.C., he reorganized the government.

Darius thought that smaller units would be easier to rule. So he divided the empire into 20 separate states called **satrapies.** Each state was ruled by an official **satrap,** meaning "protector of the kingdom." A satrap was many officials rolled into one. He was tax collector, judge, chief of police, and army recruiter. Still, each satrap answered to the king.

How did the king maintain his power? He depended upon his troops. This army was unlike that of Greek city-states. In Athens, regular citizens defended their homeland. In contrast, Persia's soldiers were full-time, paid professionals. This large army included 10,000 soldiers who were specially trained to guard the king.

READING ESSENTIALS AND STUDY GUIDE 7-3 (continued)

The Persian Religion The Persian religion was called **Zoroastri-anism.** Its founder was Zoroaster, who believed in one god. Zoroaster began preaching after seeing <u>visions</u>. He preached that this supreme being created all things. His god was a force for goodness. But Zoroaster recognized that the world contained evil. It was up to each human to choose between good and evil, and right and wrong. This religion still has followers today.

Academic Vocabulary
vision: picture created by the imagination (p. 353)

8. What prompted Persian rulers to build roads?

_____

_____

The Persian Wars (pages 354–357)

(Main Idea) Both Sparta and Athens played roles in defeating the Persians.

Persians often battled Greeks who set up colonies near the Mediterranean. By the mid-500s B.C., Greek cities in Asia Minor had already fallen to Persia. In 499 B.C., the Athenian army helped these cities rebel against their Persian rulers. The rebellion failed. But it prompted King Darius to make a firm resolution: The Greeks must be stopped from challenging the Persian Empire.

The Battle of Marathon In 490 B.C., Persia prepared an attack near the city-state of Athens. This was the plan—20,000 soldiers would board a fleet of Persian ships. Then they would sail across the Aegean Sea and land on the plain of Marathon. Athens was just a short distance away. They would wait for the Greeks to come and attack. Persia's plan had one slight problem—the Athenians were too smart to be fooled. They had only half the number of soldiers as the Persians. Rather than risk certain defeat, they crept into the hills that overlooked the plain. There, they watched and waited.

Finally, the Persian commander grew impatient. What if the Greeks never came? He decided to sail south and launch a direct attack. So he ordered his troops back onto the ships. His plan might have worked, but he made a big mistake. He ordered the horsemen—the strongest part of the army—to board first. From the hilltops, the Greeks waited. When the cavalry was out of fighting range, they charged down onto the plain. There, the Persian foot soldiers were waiting their turn to board. Knee-deep in the water—and surprised—they were unable to defend themselves and therefore were easily defeated.

Does the word *marathon* sound familiar? According to legend, its origin grew out of this battle. The story explains that the Greeks sent a messenger home from Marathon to Athens—about 25 miles—with news of the fight. After collapsing from exhaustion, the messenger announced, "Victory." Then he died. Modern marathon races, which are about 26 miles long, are named for this famous run.

Another Persian Strike When Darius's son Xerxes became king of Persia in 486 B.C., he vowed revenge against the Greeks. In 480 B.C., he launched a new invasion. This time, the Persians sent 180,000 troops, with thousands of warships and supply boats. To defend themselves, the Greeks joined forces. Sparta sent the most soldiers, with King Leonidas as commander. Athens provided the navy. Themistocles, an Athenian general, came up with a battle plan.

The Greeks knew that the huge Persian army depended on supply boats for food. The Greeks' best chance would be to attack Persian ships and cut off the army's source of food. The Greeks needed time to ready their fleet for battle. So they stalled the Persian army, blocking it at the narrow mountain pass of Thermopylae. This place was easy to defend. So for two days, a mere 7,000 Greek soldiers held off the Persians.

But a traitor spoiled the plan for the Greeks. Directing the Persians to a mountain path, he led them around the Greeks. From there, the Persians mounted a rear attack. King Leonidas was able to send most of his troops to safety. But he and a few hundred others stayed behind and fought to the death. The Greeks lost the battle at Thermopylae. Still, they gave Athens enough time to ready 200 ships for the broader fight.

READING ESSENTIALS AND STUDY GUIDE 7-3 (continued)

Now, the Greek fleet attacked the Persian fleet in the strait of Salamis, near Athens. A strait is a narrow strip of water between two pieces of land. The Greeks knew they would have the upper hand in a naval battle. Their ships were smaller, faster, and easier to steer. So they were able to move in and around the big Persian ships. After a fierce battle, the Greeks destroyed almost the entire Persian fleet.

On land, Persian troops reached Athens. The Greeks had already fled. So the Persians burned the city. This act actually made the Greeks stronger. In 479 B.C., they united to form the largest Greek army ever. These soldiers had solid body armor, longer spears, and better training. At Plataea, northwest of Athens, they crushed the Persian army.

This battle was a turning point for the Greeks. It convinced the Persians to retreat to Asia Minor. By working together, the city-states had saved Greece from invasion.

What Caused the Persian Empire to Fall? <u>Internal</u> problems plagued the Persian Empire. The rulers who followed Darius and Xerxes raised taxes. Gold and silver flowed into the treasuries. The kings spent these riches on luxuries for the royal court. This caused anger and rebellion.

At the same time, the Persian royal family fought over who was to be king. Many of the later kings were killed by power-hungry family members. Persian kings had many wives and children. The sons had little power, and constantly plotted to take over the throne. Six of the nine rulers after Darius were murdered.

These problems left Persia open to attack. In 334 B.C., a young Greek conqueror named Alexander the Great invaded the empire. The Persians were no match for his troops. By 330 B.C., the last Persian king was dead and Alexander ruled over all his lands.

Academic Vocabulary

internal: the inside structure of a community, government, or body (p. 357)

9. What two factors weakened the Persian Empire?

_____

_____

READING ESSENTIALS AND STUDY GUIDE 7-4

The Age of Pericles *For use with pages 358–367*

Content Vocabulary

direct democracy: citizens decide government matters at mass meetings (page 359)

representative democracy: citizens choose a smaller group to govern on their behalf (page 359)

philosopher: thinkers who study questions about life (page 360)

Drawing From Experience

Suppose you are given a task—a school or community project, for example. What is the best way to get things done? Groups provide more workers and a variety of ideas. But when you do something yourself, you can skip meetings and work faster.

In this section, you will learn how Greek city-states confronted and resolved these kinds of questions.

WH6.4 Students analyze the geographic, political, economic, religious, and social structures of the early civilizations of Ancient Greece.

Focuses on:

WH6.4.2, WH6.4.3, WH6.4.6

Organizing Your Thoughts

Use the following chart to summarize what Athens was like during the Age of Pericles. Use details from the text to help you.

Government	1.
Economy	2.
Culture	3.
Wars	4.

The Athenian Empire (pages 359–360)

Main Idea Under Pericles, Athens became very powerful and more democratic.

As you read in Section 3, in 479 B.C., Persia retreated from Greece at the Battle of Plataea. Still, the empire remained a threat. So one year later, Athens joined with other city-states—except Sparta—in the Delian League.

At first, the league was headquartered on the island of Delos. However, its chief officers and most of its troops were from Athens. Soon, Athens gained further control. Before long, the purpose of the Delian League changed. No longer a partnership to fight Persia, it became an Athenian empire. Key offices moved from Delos to Athens. By 454 B.C., the Athenians began sending troops to other city-states to help common people rebel against the nobles.

Democracy in Athens Athenians believed strongly in their system of government, **direct democracy.** In a direct democracy, people decide laws and policies at mass meetings. Can you imagine this in the United States? How impossible would a mass meeting of 290 million citizens be? Our system is a **representative democracy.** Under this type of government, citizens choose a smaller group to make governmental decisions on their behalf. With a large population, this system makes practical sense.

Direct democracy worked in Athens because of its small size. In the mid-400s B.C., about 43,000 male citizens over 18 years old made up the assembly. This body passed laws, elected officials, and made military decisions. Usually, fewer than 6,000 attended meetings, which took place every 10 days. Ten officials known as generals carried out the assembly's policies.

Academic Vocabulary

behalf: to represent or support another person (p. 359)

READING ESSENTIALS AND STUDY GUIDE 7-4 (continued)

The Achievements of Pericles After the Persian Wars, a general named Pericles became Athens' greatest statesman. Pericles guided Athens for more than 30 years—from his election in 461 B.C. to just before his death in 429 B.C.

Pericles helped Athens control the Delian League. He treated the other city-states like subjects. He demanded strict loyalty and steady payments. He even insisted they use Athenian coins and units of measure.

Meanwhile, Pericles made Athens itself more democratic. He believed that people's talents mattered more than social standing. So he allowed lower-class citizens to run for office. For the first time, poor citizens could become part of government's inner circle.

Pericles began a major reconstruction program. New statues, temples, and other structures were built to replace those destroyed by war. Culture also blossomed under the Age of Pericles. Creativity and learning flourished. Pericles supported artists, architects, and writers. He promoted **philosophers**—people who study questions about life. Pericles worked to make sure that Athens lived up to the name he gave it—"the school of Greece."

5. Name at least three ways that Pericles improved life for the citizens of Athens.

_____

_____

READING ESSENTIALS AND STUDY GUIDE 7-4 (continued)

Daily Life in Athens (pages 362–363)

Main Idea) Athenian men and women had very different roles.

In the 400s B.C., more people lived in Athens than in any other Greek city-state. The following breakdown shows the different population segments of Athens:

• Citizens	150,000
• Foreigners	35,000
• Slaves	100,000
Total residents	285,000

Roles of Men and Women The lives of Athenian men and women were quite different. Men usually worked in the morning, then exercised or went to meetings. In the evenings, upper-class men enjoyed all-male gatherings where they drank, dined, and discussed politics or philosophy.

The life of Athenian women centered on the home. Girls married at age 14 or 15. They were expected to have children and take care of the household. Poor women might also work alongside their husbands in the fields. Some sold goods in the agora. Upper-class women stayed at home. There, they supervised servants and made cloth—spinning, dyeing, and weaving it. They rarely left the house. Even when they went to funerals or festivals, a male relative had to accompany them.

Even though Athenian women could not attend school, many learned to read and play music. Still, they could not own property or have political rights. Even educated women were not considered equal to men.

A few women moved more freely in public life. One famous example is Aspasia, a well-educated woman. The fact that she was not a native Athenian gave her special status. She could not vote or hold office. Still, she

READING ESSENTIALS AND STUDY GUIDE 7-4 (continued)

managed to influence politics indirectly. Aspasia taught public speaking to many Athenians. Leaders—including Pericles—often consulted with her. Her writings have not survived. Yet Plato, the famous Greek philosopher, claimed her work helped shape his ideas.

Slavery in Athens Even in great democracies like Athens, slavery was common. Most Athenian homes had at least one enslaved person. Rich Athenian families had many. Often the enslaved people had been captured by the Athenians during battle with non-Greeks.

The roles of enslaved men and women were different. Men usually did heavy labor. Women became cooks and maids. Sometimes educated slaves became tutors to children. Others worked in artisans' shops or in the fields. Enslaved people were treated differently, depending on where they worked. A few held privileged positions, such as being an overseer on a farm.

Athens grew dependent on enslaved labor. Without enslaved persons, the Athens <u>economy</u> would not have thrived.

What Drove the Athenian Economy? Many Athenians farmed for a living. Herders raised sheep and goats for wool, milk, and cheese. Some farmers grew grains, vegetables, and fruit for local use. Others grew grapes and olives to make wine and olive oil, two products sold abroad.

Athens did not have enough farmland to grow crops to support all its people. So the city had to import grain. During the 400s B.C., Athens became the trading center of Greece. Merchants and artisans grew rich making and selling pottery, jewelry, and leather goods.

> **Academic Vocabulary**
>
> **economy:** organized way in which people produce, sell, and buy goods and services (p. 363)

6. How were Athenian women unequal members of society?

_____

_____

The Peloponnesian War (pages 364–367)

Main Idea Sparta and Athens went to war for control of Greece.

As the Athenian empire became rich, other city-states grew suspicious. Led by Sparta, they joined forces against Athens. Sparta and Athens had built different kinds of societies. Neither state understood or trusted the other. Sparta and its allies believed Athens was too hostile. This led to several clashes.

Conflict Between Athens and Sparta A major earthquake and the helots' revolt had weakened Sparta. At the same time, Athens continued to increase its control. Between 460 B.C. and 450 B.C. Athens gained land near Thebes and Corinth. Both Thebes and Corinth were distrustful of Athens and got out from under Athens' control by 446 B.C. Thebes and Corinth then became allies of Sparta.

The Athenians continued to be aggressive, often fighting with other Greeks nearby. Sparta was angry over Athens' domineering spirit, and in 433 B.C., Athens' actions clashed sharply with Sparta. Finally, war broke out in 431 B.C. It dragged on until 404 B.C. Now, any possibility for future cooperation was gone. Historians call this conflict the Peloponnesian War.

Pericles' Funeral Oration During the first winter of the war, Athens held a public funeral to honor its war dead. Relatives wept for their loved ones. All the citizenry joined in a procession. Pericles addressed the crowd. He spoke about Athens' greatness and reminded people it was citizens themselves who made their government strong. This famous speech was called the Funeral Oration.

On that day, Pericles reminded Athenians that they belonged to a community. They accepted certain duties, such as paying taxes and defending the city. They also enjoyed certain rights, such as the ability to vote and run for office. As citizens, they agreed to obey the rules of their constitution—their <u>framework</u> of government.

Academic Vocabulary

framework: basic structure of a building or organization (p. 365)

READING ESSENTIALS AND STUDY GUIDE 7–4 (continued)

Pericles' speech reminded Athenians of the power of democracy. His words gave them the courage to keep fighting. His ideas still ring true for people in democratic nations today.

Why Was Athens Defeated? As the Peloponnesian War began, both Sparta and Athens thought they knew how to win. The strategy Sparta and its allies used was to surround Athens. They hoped Athens would send its army out to fight. However, Pericles knew that Athens did not fight best in open battles. So he urged farmers and others to move inside the safety of the city walls. While the Athenians stayed inside the walls, their navy delivered supplies from its colonies and allies. Sparta did not have a navy, so it could not attack the Athenian ships.

This strategy worked for Athens—for a brief time. Then, in the second year of the war, disease spread through the overcrowded city. It killed more than a third of the people, including Pericles himself in 429 B.C. Still, Athens fought on. The standoff continued for another 25 years.

It was Sparta that changed the standoff. Desperate to win, Spartans made a deal with the Persian Empire, their former enemy. In exchange for money, they gave Persia some Greek territory in Asia Minor. With the money, they built a navy.

In 405 B.C., Sparta's new navy destroyed the Athenian fleet. The next year, Athens lost many land battles. So they surrendered. The Spartans and their allies tore down the city walls and broke up the Athenian empire. The long war was over.

The Results of the War The Peloponnesian War weakened all the Greek city-states—both winners and losers. Many people died fighting. Many farms were destroyed, and thousands lost their jobs. The war also made it impossible for the Greeks to work together again.

READING ESSENTIALS AND STUDY GUIDE 7-4 (continued)

After defeating Athens, Sparta tried to rule all of Greece. Within 30 years, however, the city-states rebelled. A new war began. As they fought amongst themselves, the Greeks failed to look beyond their own borders. If they had, they might have noticed a greater threat. To their north, the kingdom of Macedonia was growing in power.

This mistake would cost Greece its freedom.

7. Why did Sparta seek support from the Persian Empire?

_____

_____

READING ESSENTIALS AND STUDY GUIDE 8-1

The Culture of Ancient Greece   *For use with pages 376–385*

Content Vocabulary

myth: a traditional story about gods and heroes (page 377)

oracle: a holy shrine where a priest or priestess spoke for the god or goddess (page 378)

epic: a long poem about heroes and heroines (page 379)

fable: a short story that teaches a lesson (page 380)

drama: a story told by actors who pretend to be characters in the story (page 382)

tragedy: a drama, or story, with an unhappy ending (page 382)

comedy: a drama, or story, with a happy ending (page 383)

Drawing From Experience

Do you believe that a god throws the lightning bolts during a thunderstorm? Probably not—today, science explains many things about nature and life.

In this section you will learn how the ancient Greeks used stories about the gods to explain many things about nature and life.

Organizing Your Thoughts

Use the following table to see how the five types of Greek stories are similar and different. Use details from the text to help you fill in each blank. Use **A** for always, **S** for sometimes, and **N** for never.

WH6.4 Students analyze the geographic, political, economic, religious, and social structures of the early civilizations of Ancient Greece.

Focuses on:
WH6.4.4, WH6.4.8

Story Characteristics	Myth	Epic Poem	Fable	Drama–Tragedy	Drama–Comedy
The main character is a hero or god.	1.	2.	3.	4.	5.
The story has a moral or point.	6.	7.	8.	9.	10.
The story is short.	11.	12.	13.	14.	15.
The story is funny or has a happy ending.	16.	17.	18.	19.	20.

Reading Essentials and Study Guide 8-1 (continued)

Greek Mythology (pages 377–378)

Main Idea The Greeks believed that gods and goddesses controlled nature and shaped their lives.

The Greeks believed in many gods and goddesses. The Greeks told myths about their gods. **Myths** are traditional stories about gods and heroes. The Greeks believed the gods affected everyday life. That is why every city built beautiful temples to the gods. The Greeks hoped the temples would make the gods happy because happy gods would not hurt the city.

Greek Gods and Goddesses The Greeks believed that the gods controlled nature. The god Zeus ruled the sky and threw lightning bolts. The goddess Demeter made the crops grow. Poseidon—one of Zeus's brothers—ruled the sea and caused earthquakes.

The most important gods lived on Mount Olympus, the highest mountain in Greece. They lived above the clouds, where no human could see them.

Greek gods were not thought to be all-powerful. In many ways, gods were like humans with special powers. The gods got married, had children, made friends and enemies, fought with each other, and played tricks on one another.

To convince the gods to be kind and <u>grant</u> good fortune, the Greeks had festivals of the gods and performed religious rituals, or ceremonies. This included special prayers and giving gifts to the gods.

The Greeks also believed in an afterlife. The spirits of the dead lived beneath the earth and were ruled by Hades.

What Was a Greek Oracle? The Greeks believed that everyone had a fate, or destiny. They also thought that the gods made prophecies, or predictions, to help people plan for the future. People who wanted to know the future, or listen to other advice, visited an **oracle.** An oracle is a holy shrine where a priest or priestess talks to one of the gods. People asked the priestess questions. She told

Academic Vocabulary
grant: to permit as a favor (p. 378)

READING ESSENTIALS AND STUDY GUIDE 8-1 (continued)

her answers to the priests. Then the priests translated the answers.

Many answers were riddles. Once King Croesus asked if he should go to war against the Persians. The oracle said that if Croesus attacked the Persians, he would destroy a mighty empire. Croesus attacked, but the Persian army crushed his army. It turned out that Croesus's own—"mighty empire"—was destroyed!

21. Why did the Greeks have festivals and rituals for their gods?

_____

_____

Greek Poetry and Fables (pages 379–380)

Main Idea Greek poetry and fables taught Greek values.

Greek poems and stories are the oldest in the Western world. Many writers have copied ideas from these old stories.

The earliest Greek stories were called **epics.** Epics are long poems about heroic deeds. Two great epics are the *Iliad* and the *Odyssey*. Homer wrote them both in the 700s B.C. They tell about a war between cities in Greece and the city of Troy.

In the *Iliad*, a prince of Troy kidnaps Helen, the wife of the king of Sparta. The result is a battle to capture Troy. The Greeks eventually capture the city and win the war.

The *Odyssey* tells the story of Odysseus, a Greek hero at Troy. On his trip home from the Trojan War, Odysseus faces storms, giants, and witches. It takes him 10 years to get home, which is why we call a long journey with adventures an *odyssey*.

The Greeks believed that the *Iliad* and *Odyssey* were not just stories. They thought the epics were real history.

READING ESSENTIALS AND STUDY GUIDE 8-1 (continued)

These poems gave the Greeks a history filled with heroes and brave deeds. <u>Generations</u> of Greeks read Homer's works. Homer's epic poems taught that friendship and marriage should be valued. Homer's heroes became role models for Greek boys.

Who Was Aesop? About 550 B.C., there was a Greek slave called Aesop. He made up **fables,** or short tales that teach a lesson. In most of Aesop's fables, animals talk and act like people. Fables always have a point, or moral. Fables point out human flaws as well as strengths.

One of Aesop's best-known fables is "The Tortoise and the Hare." In it, a tortoise, or turtle, challenges a hare, or rabbit, to a race. Halfway through the race, the hare is ahead. The hare stops to rest and falls asleep. As the hare oversleeps, the tortoise continues at a slow but steady pace and wins the race.

The moral of that fable is "slow and steady wins the race." Today, we still use sayings from Aesop's fables. Aesop's fables were part of Greece's oral <u>tradition</u> for about 200 years. That means that people told the stories out loud. Eventually, people started writing down the fables. Since then, fables have been retold in many languages.

Academic Vocabulary
generation: a group of individuals born and living at the same time in history (p. 380)

Academic Vocabulary
tradition: the handing down of information, beliefs, or customs from one generation to another (p. 380)

22. What are the characteristics of a fable?

_____

_____

Greek Drama *(pages 382–383)*

Main Idea Greek drama still shapes entertainment today.

A **drama** is a story told by actors who pretend to be characters in the story. They speak, show emotion, and imitate the actions of those characters. Movies, plays, and television shows are all drama. Greek dramas dealt with big questions, such as the nature of good and evil, the rights of people, and the role of gods in everyday life.

READING ESSENTIALS AND STUDY GUIDE 8-1 (continued)

Tragedies and Comedies The Greeks put on plays during religious festivals in outdoor theaters.

The Greeks developed two types of drama—**tragedy** and **comedy.** A tragedy has an unhappy ending. People cannot solve their problems no matter how hard they try. Early Greek tragedies were about people who fought against fate. Later tragedies were about people who made bad personal choices.

A comedy ends happily. Today we use *comedy* to mean a funny story. But comedy actually means any story with a happy ending.

Aeschylus, Sophocles, and Euripides wrote tragedies. Aristophanes wrote comedies.

Early Greek plays had only one actor. The actor stood on a bare stage and gave speeches. A chorus stood behind the actor and sang songs to describe what was happening. Aeschylus was the first to add a second actor to his plays. This let him write a story about <u>conflict</u> between two people. Aeschylus also added costumes, props, and stage decorations.

In 458 B.C., Aeschylus wrote a group of three plays called the *Oresteia.* They describe what happened when the king of Mycenae returns after the Trojan War. The *Oresteia* teaches that evil acts can cause more evil acts. The moral of the plays is that people should not try to get revenge.

Euripides wrote after Aeschylus and Sophocles. Euripides wrote about everyday people. He challenged traditional thinking. He showed war as cruel.

The comedies of Aristophanes poked fun at politicians and local scholars. Aristophanes' plays included jokes, and they encouraged the audience to think while they laughed.

Academic Vocabulary
conflict: strong disagreement (p. 383)

23. What two types of drama did the Greeks create?

_____

_____

READING ESSENTIALS AND STUDY GUIDE 8-1 (continued)

Greek Art and Architecture *(pages 384–385)*

Main Idea Greek art and architecture expressed Greek ideas of beauty and harmony.

Greek artists hoped that their art would help teach people about reason, moderation, balance, and harmony. Greek artists painted murals and made pottery. Large vases often have pictures from myths. Small pieces, like cups, have pictures from everyday life.

The Greeks were also skilled architects—people who design buildings. The most important buildings were the temples, like the Parthenon. Temples contained rooms that housed statues of the gods and the gifts that people offered to the gods.

Large columns supported the roofs of Greek buildings. At first, the columns were made of wood. Then, in 500 B.C., they were marble, or stone. We still use marble columns in churches and large buildings today. For example, the White House and the Capitol building both have columns.

Many Greek temples were decorated with sculpture. Sculpture, like all of Greek art, expressed ideas. Greek artists liked to copy the human body, but they did not copy it exactly. They did not include flaws. Instead, artists tried to show their ideas of perfection and beauty.

24. What was the most important type of building in ancient Greece?

_____

_____

READING ESSENTIALS AND STUDY GUIDE 8-2

Greek Philosophy and History   *For use with pages 392–397*

Content Vocabulary

philosophy: comes from the Greek word for "love of wisdom" (page 393)

philosophers: Greek thinkers who believed that people could understand everything by studying and thinking about it (page 393)

Sophist: professional teacher in ancient Greece (page 393)

Socratic method: a way of teaching in which the teacher asks students questions that make the students use logic to figure out things (page 394)

Drawing From Experience

Most of us have done something, and then realized that we really had not thought about it first. Sometimes we get into trouble or hurt someone's feelings.

In the last section you learned how the ancient Greeks used stories about the gods to explain many things about nature and life.

Organizing Your Thoughts

In this section you will read about Greek philosophers and historians. They are the Sophists, Socrates, Aristotle, Plato, Herodotus, and Thucydides.

In the box next to each name, write an important fact about the person or group. Use details from the text to help you fill in each box.

WH6.4 Students analyze the geographic, political, economic, religious, and social structures of the early civilizations of Ancient Greece.

Focuses on:

WH6.4.8

Name	Facts
1. Sophists	
2. Socrates	
3. Plato	
4. Aristotle	
5. Herodotus	
6. Thucydides	

READING ESSENTIALS AND STUDY GUIDE 8-2 (continued)

Greek Philosophers (pages 393–395)

Main Idea Greek philosophers developed ideas that are still used today.

The word **philosophy** means "love of wisdom." The first **philosophers** were Greek thinkers. They thought that people could understand everything. Greek philosophy led to the study of history, political science, science, and mathematics.

Many philosophers were teachers. Pythagoras was one of them. He taught that numbers could describe all the relationships in the world. He invented the Pythagorean theorem, which helps us figure out how long the sides of a triangle are.

Who Were the Sophists? The **Sophists** were teachers in ancient Greece. They thought that students should improve themselves by reading and thinking. Sophists taught how to make good arguments and political speeches.

Sophists did not believe that the gods influenced everyday life. They also <u>rejected</u> the concept of "absolute" right or wrong. They thought that a thing could be wrong for one person and right for another.

> **Academic Vocabulary**
>
> **reject:** to refuse to believe (p. 394)

The Ideas of Socrates Socrates was a sculptor in Athens. He loved philosophy but left no writings behind. We know about him from his students' writings.

Socrates did not agree with the Sophists. He thought there was an absolute right and wrong. He thought that everybody already knows everything. The knowledge was buried deep inside each person.

Socrates believed that absolute truth existed. Socrates tried to help people find the knowledge inside themselves through the **Socratic method** of teaching. In this method, he asked his pupils hard questions, forcing them to use their reason to answer these questions.

Some leaders in Athens thought Socrates was dangerous. He encouraged people to question their leaders' decisions. In 399 B.C., Socrates was arrested and found guilty of teaching his students to rebel. He was sentenced to death.

READING ESSENTIALS AND STUDY GUIDE 8-2 (continued)

Socrates could have left Athens, but he refused to do so. He said that he lived in Athens, so he had to obey the city's laws. He drank poison to carry out his death sentence.

The Ideas of Plato Plato was one of Socrates' students. He wrote a book called the *Republic*. Plato did not like democracy. His ideal government divided people into three groups.

The top group was philosopher-kings. Philosopher-kings ruled with wisdom and logic. The second group was warriors. They protected the kingdom with their courage. The third group was everyone else. Plato thought they were not wise or brave. So they did all of the other jobs in the kingdom.

Unlike most men at that time, Plato believed that women should also be educated and be allowed to do the same jobs as men.

Who Was Aristotle? Plato started a school in Athens. It was called the Academy. His best student was Aristotle. Aristotle wrote more than 200 books on government, science, and the planets.

In 355 B.C., Aristotle opened his own school called the Lyceum. Aristotle taught his students the "golden mean." This idea says that people should not do too much of something.

Aristotle told his students to see, or observe, the world around them. He was the first person to separate his observations by similarities and differences. For example, some animals fly, and others do not. Then he made generalizations based on groups of facts.

Aristotle also wrote about government in *Politics*. He studied the governments of 158 different places and divided them into three types:

- Government by one person, such as a king or queen, or a tyrant

READING ESSENTIALS AND STUDY GUIDE 8-2 (continued)

- Government by a few people, such as an aristocracy or an oligarchy
- Government by many people, such as a democracy

Aristotle thought that the best government was a combination of oligarchy and democracy. The United States tries to combine these types of government.

7. How were Aristotle's ideas on government different from Plato's?

_____

_____

Greek Historians (page 397)

Main Idea) Greeks wrote the first real histories in Western civilization.

For thousands of years, people did not write history. They used legends and myths to explain their past. Some civilizations kept lists of rulers. But no one wrote down events. Then, in 435 B.C., Herodotus wrote a history book about the Persian Wars. He tried to separate fact from legend and is the first person to record events as they happened. Today, many historians call him the "father of history."

Thucydides is thought to be the greatest historian of the ancient world. He said that humans, not gods, were responsible for wars and politics. Thucydides fought in the Peloponnesian War. Afterward, he wrote *History of the Peloponnesian War*. Thucydides wrote only about what he saw or what eyewitnesses saw. He stressed the importance of having <u>accurate</u> facts.

Academic Vocabulary
accurate: to be free from mistakes (p. 397)

8. Who did Thucydides think was responsible for war and politics?

_____

_____

Reading Essentials and Study Guide 8-3

Alexander the Great *For use with pages 398–403*

Content Vocabulary

legacy: what a person leaves behind when he or she dies (page 402)

Hellenistic Era: a time when Greek ideas and the Greek language spread to non-Greek people (page 402)

Drawing From Experience

Think about the last time you did a project with school, a club, or a religious group. Could everyone suggest ideas? Good leaders—of projects, groups, and nations—try to use good ideas, no matter where they come from.

In the last section you learned about Greek thinkers and historians. In this section, you will learn about how Alexander the Great spread Greek culture.

WH6.4 Students analyze the geographic, political, economic, religious, and social structures of the early civilizations of Ancient Greece.

Focuses on:
WH6.4.7

Organizing Your Thoughts

Philip II of Macedonia started building an empire. Alexander the Great finished it. In the time line below, write what they did. Use details from the text to help you.

1. In 359 B.C., Philip _____

2. In 338 B.C., Philip _____

3. In 334 B.C., Alexander _____

4. In 332 B.C., Alexander _____

5. In 326 B.C., Alexander _____

6. In 323 B.C., Alexander _____

Macedonia Attacks Greece (pages 399–400)

`Main Idea` Philip II of Macedonia united the Greek states.

Macedonia lay north of Greece. The people were warriors. They raised sheep and horses, and farmed. By 400 B.C., Macedonia was almost as powerful as the Greek city-states.

A Plan to Win Greece In 359 B.C., Philip II became king of Macedonia. He wanted to defeat the Persian Empire. In order to achieve this goal, he needed to increase Macedonia's strength. Philip trained his army to fight like the Greek hoplites. Then, one by one, he took over the Greek city-states.

> **Academic Vocabulary**
>
> **achieve:** to get something desired by effort (p. 399)

Demosthenes was a lawyer and one of Athens's great public speakers. He warned that Philip threatened their freedom. He urged Athens and other city-states to fight the Macedonians. But the Greeks were weak and divided from the Peloponnesian War. Thousands of Greek men joined the Persian army. The city-states were weak.

This was good news for Philip. The Athenians tried to fight Philip's army, but they could not stop him. In 338 B.C., the Macedonians crushed the Greeks at the Battle of Chaeronea near Thebes. Philip now controlled all of Greece.

7. Why did Philip II invade Greece?

_____

_____

Alexander Builds an Empire (pages 400–403)

`Main Idea` Alexander the Great conquered the Persian Empire and spread Greek culture throughout southwest Asia.

Before Philip could conquer the Persian Empire, he was murdered. His son Alexander took over as king of Macedonia. Alexander was only 20, but he had already been in battle many times.

READING ESSENTIALS AND STUDY GUIDE 8-3 (continued)

What Did Alexander Conquer? Alexander invaded Asia Minor in 334 B.C. He had about 37,000 foot soldiers and 5,000 warriors on horseback. At the Battle of Granicus, he destroyed the local Persian army.

At that time, the Persians ruled many Greek cities in Asia Minor. During the next nine months, Alexander freed those city-states. He also defeated a large Persian army at Issus.

Then Alexander went south. By the winter of 332 B.C., he had captured Egypt and Syria. He built the city of Alexandria in Egypt. It became famous for trade, science, and education. In 331 B.C. Alexander went east. He defeated the Persians at Guagamela, near Babylon. Then his army took over the rest of the Persian Empire. His father's dream was fulfilled.

But Alexander did not stop. He marched east for the next three years. His army got as far as modern Pakistan. In 326 B.C. Alexander and his army crossed the Indus River and fought many battles in India. His soldiers grew tired of war, so Alexander agreed to go home.

Going home, the army crossed a desert in what is modern Iran. There was very little water. Heat and thirst killed thousands of soldiers. When soldiers found some water, they gave it to Alexander in a helmet. Alexander poured the water on the ground. He showed his soldiers that he was willing to suffer the same thirst and pain that they did.

Alexander arrived back in Babylon in 323 B.C. He wanted to invade southern Arabia, but he died 10 days later. He was 32.

Alexander's Legacy Alexander was a great and brave <u>military</u> leader. Sometimes he rode into battle before his army. Some considered this foolish, but his bravery inspired his soldiers. Alexander always tried to copy his hero Achilles. Achilles was one of the warriors in the *Iliad* by Homer.

When he died, Alexander was the most powerful ruler in the ancient world. That is one reason we call him Alexander the Great.

Academic Vocabulary
military: an army (p. 401)

READING ESSENTIALS AND STUDY GUIDE 8-3 (continued)

A **legacy** is what a person leaves to other people when he or she dies. Alexander's legacy was a world that knew about Greek culture. Wherever Alexander and his army went, they spread the Greek language, ideas, and art. This is another reason that Alexander is "the Great." Alexander also learned things in Asia and Africa. He brought those ideas back to Greece.

Alexander began the **Hellenistic Era.** *Hellenistic* means "like the Greeks." The Hellenistic Era is the time when Greek ideas spread to people who were not Greek.

The Empire Breaks Apart Alexander wanted the Macedonians, the Greeks, and the Persians to become one people. He used Persians as local officials and encouraged his soldiers to marry Asian women.

After Alexander died, the empire fell apart. It became four Hellenistic kingdoms: Macedonia, Pergamum, Egypt, and the Seleucid Empire. Greek was the official language of these kingdoms. And the kings often gave jobs to Greeks or Macedonians.

By 100 B.C., Alexandria was the largest city in the Mediterranean world. The Hellenistic kings built many other cities, too. These cities needed many workers. They needed architects and engineers. They also needed philosophers, artists, and artisans. The kings asked Greeks and Macedonians to move to these cities. These colonists helped spread the Greek culture into Egypt and as far east as modern Afghanistan and India.

8. What was Alexander's legacy?

_____

_____

READING ESSENTIALS AND STUDY GUIDE 8-4

The Spread of Greek Culture *For use with pages 406–411*

Content Vocabulary

Epicureanism: a philosophy that teaches that people are happy if they spend time with friends and do not worry (page 408)

Stoicism: a philosophy that teaches that people are happy if they do their duty and follow logic, not emotion (page 408)

astronomers: people who study stars, planets, and other heavenly bodies (page 409)

plane geometry: branch of mathematics that shows how points, lines, angles, and surfaces, or planes, relate to each other (page 410)

solid geometry: branch of mathematics that studies spheres, or balls, and cylinders, or tubes (page 410)

Drawing From Experience

Suppose you are given a task—a school or community project, for example. What is the best way to get things done? Groups provide more workers and a variety of ideas. But when you do something yourself, you can skip meetings and work faster.

The last section described how Alexander the Great spread Greek culture. In this section, you will learn how the kings after Alexander supported learning and new ideas in philosophy, science, math, and astronomy.

WH6.4 Students analyze the geographic, political, economic, religious, and social structures of the early civilizations of Ancient Greece.

Focuses on:

WH6.4.7, WH6.4.8

Organizing Your Thoughts

The Epicureans and the Stoics were philosophers. What were their beliefs? Use details from the text to help you fill in the table. Place **Y** for yes and **N** for no in the appropriate box.

Philosophy	Happiness Is Life's Goal	People Should Ignore Emotions	People Should Be in Politics	People Should Not be in Politics	Doing Your Duty Makes You Happy	Friends Make You Happy
Epicurean	1.	2.	3.	4.	5.	6.
Stoic	7.	8.	9.	10.	11.	12.

Greek Culture Spreads *(page 407)*

Main Idea Hellenistic cities became centers of learning and culture.

Thousands of scientists, writers, philosophers, and others came to the Hellenistic cities. Many came to use Alexandria's library or to study literature, languages, and science.

Architecture and Sculpture Greek architects helped design the new cities and rebuild the old ones. The kings wanted Greek baths, temples, and theaters. The kings and other rich citizens hired Greek sculptors to make statues as good as any Greek statues.

Literature and Theater Writers wrote drama, poetry, and histories at this time, but most of it has been lost or destroyed. Appolonius of Rhodes wrote an epic poem called *Argonautica.* It is about Jason and his crew and their adventures. Another poet, Theocritus, wrote short poems about nature and its beauty.

Athens was still the center of Greek drama. Playwrights in Athens invented a new kind of comedy that told about love and people. Menander was the best-known of these new playwrights. He lived from 343 B.C. to 291 B.C.

13. How did the Hellenistic kings spread Greek culture?

_____

_____

New Philosophy and Science *(pages 408–410)*

Main Idea Philosophers and scientists in the Hellenistic Era introduced new ideas and made major discoveries.

During this time, the most famous philosophers still went to Athens. The two most important philosophers at this time were Epicurus and Zeno.

Epicureans Epicurus developed **Epicureanism.** This philosophy taught people that happiness is the goal of life. Today, *epicurean* means a love of fine foods and comfortable things. To Epicurus, happiness meant spending time with friends and not worrying. He said that people should stay out of politics and public service.

Who Were the Stoics? Zeno developed **Stoicism.** He taught at a building called the "painted porch." Since the Greek word for porch is *stoa,* his school was called the stoics. Zeno could not afford a lecture hall.

Stoics thought that happiness came from following logic and reason. Emotions like anger or sadness caused problems. Today we call people stoics if they keep going even if they are hurt or sad. Stoics also thought that people were happy when they did their duty. They should be in politics and public service.

Greek Science and Math Scientists made major contributions during the Hellenistic Era. Aristarchus was an astronomer. **Astronomers** study stars, planets, and other heavenly bodies. Aristarchus said that the sun was at the center of the universe. He said that Earth went around the sun. No one believed him. They thought that the sun went around the earth.

Eratosthenes was an astronomer in charge of Alexandria's library. He figured out that the earth was round and how big it was.

Here's how he did it. Eratosthenes put two sticks in the ground far apart from each other. He waited until the sun was directly over one stick. It had a shorter shadow than the other stick. After measuring the shadows, Eratosthenes used math to figure out the curve of Earth's surface.

Eratosthenes estimated that the distance around the earth was 24,675 miles. He was only 185 miles off! He also measured the distance to the sun and the moon. Both of these measurements are close.

Euclid was a mathematician who wrote *Elements.* The book teaches **plane geometry**—how points, lines, angles, and surfaces work together. Archimedes of Syracuse

Academic Vocabulary
goal: the object toward which effort is directed (p. 408)

Academic Vocabulary
lecture: a talk given in front of a group for instruction (p. 408)

Academic Vocabulary
major: great in number, quality, or extent (p. 409)

READING ESSENTIALS AND STUDY GUIDE 8-4 (continued)

worked on **solid geometry**—the study of spheres, or balls, and cylinders, or tubes. He discovered *pi,* which is used to measure circles. Its symbol is π.

The most famous scientist of the Hellenistic Era—Archimedes was also an inventor. He invented a type of lever called the catapult. Catapults are war machines that hurl rocks and arrows at the enemy.

The catapults worked well. In 212 B.C. the Romans attacked Syracuse. But they could not get past the catapults. It took the Romans three years to capture Syracuse. Finally the Romans got inside the city walls. They massacred everyone in the city, including Archimedes.

Hypatia lived in Alexandria in Egypt about A.D. 400. She followed the Greek tradition of studying philosophy and mathematics. She also wrote about astronomy. She is known as one of the first women mathematicians who recorded important information for future generations.

14. Who was the most famous scientist of the Hellenistic Era? What did he contribute?

_____

_____

Greece Falls to Rome (page 411)

Main Idea) Greek power declined as a new power in the Mediterranean arose: Rome.

Alexander's empire produced four Greek kingdoms that were often fighting. Macedonia was dominant for a long time. Other city-states like Sparta became independent. It was hard for them to remain independent, though, because they didn't have strong military forces.

A city-state named Rome grew in importance in the late 200s B.C. After conquering the Italian peninsula, Rome expanded into Greece. The Romans invaded Macedonia and divided it up. By 146 B.C. Rome controlled all of Greece.

READING ESSENTIALS AND STUDY GUIDE 9-1

Rome's Beginnings *For use with pages 420–425*

Content Vocabulary

republic: a form of government in which rulers are elected by citizens (page 423)

legion: Roman army units of 6,000 men each (page 424)

Drawing From Experience

Every day we use things and eat foods from other parts of the world. We write on paper, which the Chinese invented. We eat tacos and pizza. We play soccer and other games that came from other countries.

In this section, you will learn how Rome grew from a small city to an economic and military power.

WH6.7 Students analyze the geographic, political, economic, religious, and social structures during the development of Rome.

Focuses on:

WH6.7.1

Organizing Your Thoughts

There is a very famous saying, "Rome was not built in a day." Many different groups of people contributed to Rome. Use details from the text to help you fill in what each group contributed.

	Latins (Romans)	**Greeks**	**Etruscans**
What did they contribute to Rome?	1.	2.	3.

READING ESSENTIALS AND STUDY GUIDE 9-1 (continued)

The Origins of Rome (pages 421–423)

Main Idea Geography played an important role in the rise of Roman Civilization.

Italy is a peninsula in the Mediterranean Sea. It is shaped like a boot. The heel points toward Greece, the toe points toward the island of Sicily.

The Alps cross the top of Italy and separate it from the rest of Europe. The Apennines run from north to south. These mountains could be crossed easily. As a result, people who settled in Italy were not as <u>isolated</u> as Greek communities. This helped people in early Italy trade ideas and goods with each other. Italy has a mild climate and rich soil. Many of its lower mountains have flat tops that make good farms. With more <u>capacity</u> to produce food, Italy could support more people than Greece could.

Academic Vocabulary
isolate: to be apart from others (p. 421)

Academic Vocabulary
capacity: the ability to do something well (p. 421)

Historians do not know much about the first people in Italy. People in Europe crossed the Alps between 1500 B.C. and 1000 B.C. These people included the Latins, or the Romans. The Romans built the city of Rome.

Where Was Rome Located? Rome was built on the Tiber River. The river could be used for fresh water and transportation. And because it was built on a spot that could be crossed easily, Rome became a trading stop.

In addition, Rome was built 15 miles *up* the river from the Mediterranean Sea. That way, pirates could not attack the city. To protect it further, the Romans built Rome on seven hills.

How Did Rome Begin? Historians think that the Romans tended herds and grew crops on Rome's hills. Then around 800 B.C. to 700 B.C., they realized that they would be safer if they lived together. Their community grew into Rome.

Early Influences After 800 B.C., the Greeks and the Etruscans came to Italy. The Greeks built many colonies in Italy between 750 B.C. and 550 B.C. They taught the Romans to grow olives and grapes, and to use the Greek alphabet. Romans also copied Greek sculpture and other art forms.

╔══╗
READING ESSENTIALS AND STUDY GUIDE 9-1 (continued)
╚══╝

The Etruscans were from Etruria, which was north of Rome. At that time, Rome was a village with straw huts. But that changed after 650 B.C. when the Etruscans conquered Rome and enslaved its people. They had the enslaved people build buildings, temples, and streets around a central square.

The Etruscans introduced togas and short cloaks. A toga is like a sheet wrapped around your body, with one end thrown over your shoulder.

Most important, the Etruscans showed the Romans how an army could work. Later the Romans copied the Etruscan army and conquered an empire.

4. How did geography help the Romans prosper?

_____

_____

The Birth of a Republic (pages 423–425)

Main Idea The Romans created a republic and conquered Italy. By treating people fairly, they built Rome from a small city into a great power.

The Etruscans ruled Rome for more than 100 years. The ruling family was named the Tarquins. Under them, Rome grew very rich and strong. But they were very cruel. So in 509 B.C., the Romans rebelled and set up a **republic.** A republic is a form of government in which leaders are elected. The rise of the Roman Republic marked the beginning of a new <u>chapter</u> in Rome's history.

Rome was still a small city when it became a republic. It had enemies all around it. Over the next 200 years, Rome fought war after war. In 338 B.C., the Romans beat nearby Latin cities. In 284 B.C., the Romans beat the Etruscan cities. By 267 B.C., the Romans had taken over the Greek colonies in Italy and ruled almost all of Italy.

Why Was Rome So Strong? The Romans were great soldiers. At the beginning of the republic, every male citizen who owned land had to join the army. Men who ran away, or

Academic Vocabulary
chapter: a new division of time in history or in a book (p. 423)

READING ESSENTIALS AND STUDY GUIDE 9-1 (continued)

deserted, were killed. This turned Romans into fighters who did not give up easily.

Roman soldiers did not just fight. They thought of better ways to organize their army. For example, at first the Romans marched next to each other with shields together to block enemy arrows and spears. But this way of fighting was slow.

Then the generals divided their armies into smaller groups, called **legions.** Each legion had about 6,000 men broken into groups of 60 or 120 men. These small groups could move quickly.

Roman soldiers were called *legionaries.* They had a short sword called a *gladius* and a spear called a *pilum.* Each group also had a *standard.* A standard was a tall pole with a symbol on top. The standard would keep the groups together during battle.

Shrewd Rulers The Romans were also smart planners. They built military towns everywhere they conquered. Then they built roads to these towns. Soon their armies traveled quickly across Italy.

The Romans started the Roman Confederation. This meant that some of the people Rome conquered could become full citizens. They could vote and be in the government. They were also treated the same as other citizens by the law.

The Romans granted other peoples the <u>status</u> of allies. Allies could run their own towns, but they had to pay taxes to Rome. Allies also had to fight in Rome's armies. The Romans let the allies know that if the allies were loyal, they might become citizens.

The Romans treated the people they conquered well. They did that because people who are treated well do not rebel. If an area did rebel, Rome squashed it. As a result, the Roman republic grew stronger.

5. How did Rome rule its new conquests?

_____

_____

Academic Vocabulary
status: a position or rank (p. 425)

READING ESSENTIALS AND STUDY GUIDE 9-2

The Roman Republic *For use with pages 426–434*

Content Vocabulary

patrician: wealthy landowner and member of the ruling class in ancient Rome (page 427)

plebeian: member of the common people in ancient Rome (page 427)

consul: top government official in ancient Rome (page 428)

veto: to reject another's decision (page 428)

praetor: type of judge who interpreted the law (page 428)

dictator: someone who has complete control of the government (page 429)

Drawing From Experience

Our government is divided into three different parts: Congress, the Supreme Court, and the president.

In the previous section, you learned how Rome grew from a small city to an economic and military power. In this section, you will learn how Rome became more democratic and how it took over the Mediterranean Sea region.

WH6.7 Students analyze the geographic, political, economic, religious, and social structures during the development of Rome.

Focuses on:

WH6.7.1, WH6.7.2, WH6.7.3, WH6.7.8

Organizing Your Thoughts

Rome's republic grew more democratic over time. Use the reading to help you complete the chart showing when each group got certain rights. Put in the year, or use **A** for always and **N** for never.

Right to . . .	Plebeian Men	Patrician Men	Women
marry outside of their class	1.	2.	3.
become consuls	4.	5.	6.
be in a lawmaking body	7.	8.	9.
make laws for all Romans	10.	11.	12.

READING ESSENTIALS AND STUDY GUIDE 9-2 (continued)

Rome's Government (pages 427–429)

Main Idea Rome's republic was shaped by a struggle between wealthy landowners and regular citizens as it gradually expanded the right to vote.

There were two main social classes in early Rome: **patrician** and **plebeian.** Patricians were wealthy landowners. However, most people were plebeians—shopkeepers, artisans, and small farmers. Patricians and plebeians could not marry each other.

All patrician and plebeian men were citizens and had the right to vote. They had to pay taxes and join the army. But only patricians could be in the government.

How Did Rome's Government Work? The top government posts were the **consuls,** who served for one year. Two consuls were chosen every year. One consul headed the army. The other headed the rest of the government. If one consul made a bad decision, the other could **veto** it. This means they could reject the other's decision.

The government of the Roman Republic also included **praetors,** or judges, tax collectors, and builders.

Rome had two major <u>legislative</u> groups. They were the Senate and the Assembly of Centuries. The 300 Senators served for life. At first, they only advised the consuls. By the 200s B.C., they passed laws and set building programs. The Assembly of Centuries elected the consuls and praetors, and passed laws.

Plebeians Against Patricians At first, only patrician men could be Senators, Assembly members, or consuls. But the plebeians fought in the army and paid taxes, just like the patricians. They wanted equal rights.

So, in 494 B.C., the plebeians went on strike. They would not join the army. Many left Rome, and set up their own republic.

This scared the patricians. They <u>accommodated</u> the plebeians by allowing them to have their own representatives. In 474 B.C., the plebeians set up the Council of Plebs and elected tribunes. The tribunes told the government what the plebeians thought about issues. Later, the tribunes could veto government decisions.

Academic Vocabulary

legislate: to make law (p. 428)

Academic Vocabulary

accommodate: to provide someone with something needed or desired (p. 428)

Name_____ Date_____ Class_____

┌───┐
│ **READING ESSENTIALS AND STUDY GUIDE 9-2** (continued) │
└───┘

By 455 B.C. patricians and plebeians could marry each other, and in the 300s B.C., plebeian men could become consuls. In 287 B.C., the Council of Plebs was granted the power to pass laws for all Romans. However, a few wealthy families still held most of the power.

Who Was Cincinnatus? The Roman Republic included dictators. Today, a **dictator** is a cruel ruler who controls everything. In early Rome, the dictators were elected by the Senate when there was an emergency. As soon as the emergency ended, the dictator quit.

About 460 B.C., the Roman army was attacked. The Senators elected a farmer named Cincinnatus to be dictator. Cincinnatus gathered an army to help Rome. He and his army defeated the enemy quickly. Afterward, he went home to his farm.

13. What were the two legislative bodies in the Roman Republic?

_____

_____

Roman Law (page 431)

Main Idea The Roman Republic's legal system was based on the rule of law.

The U.S. legal system copied a lot of Rome's system of law. At first, Rome's laws were not written down. Plebeians thought that the judges agreed with the rich people too often. The plebeians demanded that the laws be written down. That way everyone could know them and make sure the judges followed the laws.

In 451 B.C., the first code of laws was written down. It was carved on bronze tablets. The bronze tablets were put in the Forum. The Forum was Rome's big marketplace.

The laws were called the Twelve Tables. They set up the idea that all citizens should be treated equally by the law. All future Roman laws were based on the Twelve Tables.

READING ESSENTIALS AND STUDY GUIDE 9-2 (continued)

The Twelve Tables were only for Roman citizens. That made problems when Rome began taking over other nations. The Romans saw that they also needed laws to protect people who were not citizens.

They made a new set of laws called the Law of Nations. It listed ideas of justice. These ideas of justice were for everyone. We still use some of these ideas today. For example, the Law of Nations said that people are seen as innocent until they are proven guilty. The Law of Nations said that judges had to study evidence before making decisions.

The Romans' main idea was that the law should treat everyone equally. This is called "the rule of law." In early Rome, this was a very new idea. Many rich people did not like it. They were used to having special privileges. In fact, many rich people were not used to obeying the law at all. The rule of law made the rich respect the rights of the poor.

The rule of law is the basis for our legal system today.

14. What principle did the Twelve Tables establish?

_____

_____

Rome Expands (pages 432–434)

Main Idea Rome slowly destroyed the Carthaginian Empire and took control of the entire Mediterranean region.

The Romans ruled most of Italy. As Rome developed its government, it faced <u>challenges</u> from abroad. Now, Rome wanted to control the trade routes, but so did Carthage.

Carthage was on the coast of North Africa. It was built around 800 B.C. by the Phoenicians who were sailors and traders. Carthage had a great trading empire. It was the largest and richest city in the western Mediterranean.

Academic Vocabulary

challenge: to face difficulties (p. 432)

The First Punic War *Punicus* is the Latin word for Phoenician. That is why the wars between Rome and Carthage are called the Punic Wars.

The First Punic War started in 264 B.C. because Rome and Carthage both wanted the island of Sicily. The Romans sent an army to Sicily. Carthage already had colonies on Sicily. The colonies fought the Roman army. The Romans did not win at first. They were used to fighting on land. But Carthage was a sea power. So Rome built a navy.

The First Punic War lasted 20 years. Finally, in 241 B.C., Rome won. Carthage had to leave Sicily and pay a huge fine to the Romans.

The Second Punic War Carthage then conquered southern Spain. The Romans helped the Spanish people rebel. So in 218 B.C., Carthage sent the great general Hannibal to attack Rome. This began the Second Punic War.

Hannibal's army landed in Spain. He had about 46,000 men, horses, and 37 elephants. He marched them across the Alps and into Italy. Cold weather and the attacks killed almost half of his men. Most of the elephants were killed, too.

Hannibal's army reached Italy in 216 B.C. They beat the Romans at Cannae and began raiding Italy. In 202 B.C., the Roman general Scipio attacked Carthage. Hannibal left to protect his own people. Finally, Scipio's army beat Hannibal's. Carthage gave Spain to Rome. Carthage also had to give up its navy and pay another huge fine. Rome now ruled the western Mediterranean.

More Conquests Carthage was no longer a military power. But it was still a rich trading center. So, in 146 B.C., Roman soldiers burned the city. More than 50,000 men, women, and children were enslaved. Legend says that the Romans spread salt on the ground. Crops cannot grow in salty earth. This was the Third Punic War. After that, Carthage was a Roman province, or district.

READING ESSENTIALS AND STUDY GUIDE 9-2 (continued)

Rome was fighting other battles, too. In 148 B.C., Rome conquered Macedonia and then in 129 B.C. gained its first province in Asia. The Romans called the Mediterranean Sea *mare nostrum*, which means "our sea."

15. How did Rome punish Carthage at the end of the Third Punic War?

_____

_____

READING ESSENTIALS AND STUDY GUIDE 9-3

The Fall of the Republic *For use with pages 435–441*

Content Vocabulary

latifundia: large farming estates (page 436)

triumvirate: a political alliance of three people (three people ruling as a team) (page 438)

Drawing From Experience

Have you ever worked on a group project that no one really wanted to do? It is hard to keep everyone working. It helps if there is a reward for hard work, such as a good grade.

In the previous section, you learned how Rome became more democratic and how it took over the Mediterranean Sea region. In this section, you will learn about Julius Caesar and Augustus and why the Roman Republic ended.

WH6.7 Students analyze the geographic, political, economic, religious, and social structures during the development of Rome.

Focuses on:

WH6.7.1, WH6.7.4

Organizing Your Thoughts

Below are some people who lived when the Roman Republic was ending. List one accomplishment for each of them.

1. **Tiberius and Gaius Gracchus** _____
2. **Marius** _____
3. **Sulla** _____
4. **Julius Caesar** _____

Trouble in the Republic *(pages 436–437)*

Main Idea The use of enslaved labor hurt farmers, increased poverty and corruption, and brought the army into politics.

Even though Rome's armies were doing well, Rome had problems at home. <u>Despite</u> some gains for the plebeians, many people became unhappy with the patricians' roles in government.

Academic Vocabulary

despite: in spite of (p. 436)

READING ESSENTIALS AND STUDY GUIDE 9-3 (continued)

Problems for Farmers By 100 B.C., the plebeian farmers were in trouble. Many could not work on their farms because they were in the army. Others had watched Hannibal ruin their small farms.

At the same time, rich Romans were buying land. They formed large farming <u>estates</u> called **latifundia.** Enslaved people from Carthage worked the land. Since there were no wages, the rich could charge less for their crops than the plebeian farmers. This ran the plebeian farmers out of business.

Many farmers sold their farms and went to the cities for work. But enslaved people did most of the work. Jobs were hard to find and did not pay much. The plebeians became very angry.

Roman politicians thought that the plebeians might riot. They started giving the poor "bread and circuses." This meant free food and shows. The "bread and circuses" won the votes of the poor.

Why Did Reform Fail? Two brothers—Tiberius and Gaius Gracchus—thought the poor should get their farms back. They asked the Senate to take public land from the rich and give it to the poor.

Many Senators did not want to give up any of their land. In 133 B.C., they killed Tiberius. Twelve years later, they killed Gaius.

The Army Enters Politics Most soldiers had joined the army because it was their duty as citizens. However, they were not paid, and they were losing their farms. In 107 B.C. a military leader named Marius became consul. He paid farmers to be soldiers and promised them land.

By paying the soldiers, they became professionals. But they no longer felt loyalty to Rome. They felt loyalty to the general who paid them.

Having a loyal army gave a general a lot of power. Generals became politicians. To keep their men's loyalty, the generals worked to pass laws that gave the soldiers land. In 82 B.C., General Sulla forced Marius and other generals out of Rome. He made himself dictator.

Academic Vocabulary
estate: a large country house on a large piece of land (p. 436)

READING ESSENTIALS AND STUDY GUIDE 9-3 (continued)

Over the next three years, Sulla made the Council of Plebs weaker and the Senate stronger. Then he retired. Sulla had shown other generals how to use their armies to grab power. For the next 50 years, civil war tore Rome apart.

5. What change did Marius make to the army?

_____

_____

Julius Caesar *(pages 438–439)*

Main Idea) **Military hero Julius Caesar seized power and made reforms.**

By 60 B.C., three men held the most power in Rome. They were three generals: Crassus, Pompey, and Julius Caesar. The three joined together in the First Triumvirate. A **triumvirate** is a political partnership of three people.

Caesar's Military Campaigns Each member of the Triumvirate had a military command. Pompey was in Spain, Crassus was in Syria, and Caesar was in Gaul.

Caesar became a hero to Rome's lower classes. But the Senators thought that he was too popular and feared he would seize power. When Crassus was killed in a battle in 53 B.C., they gave Pompey complete control of Rome. Four years later, they ordered Caesar to give up his army. Caesar knew that if he obeyed the Senate, his rivals might kill him. But if he did not obey, then he was starting a civil war against Rome.

Caesar kept his army and marched 5,000 men into Italy. Pompey tried to stop Caesar, but Caesar drove Pompey out of Italy and into Greece. Then, in 48 B.C., he destroyed Pompey's army completely.

Caesar's Rise to Power In 44 B.C., Caesar made himself dictator for life. He also filled the Senate with people who supported him. Caesar knew many reforms were needed. So he gave citizenship to the people in Rome's territories, started new colonies so that farmers and soldiers would have land, and forced patricians to hire free workers.

Caesar also created the Julian calendar. It had 12 months, 365 days, and a leap year. It was used in Europe until A.D. 1582. This is very close to our calendar today.

Caesar's supporters thought he was a strong leader who brought peace to Rome. His enemies thought that he wanted to be king. Caesar was told to "beware the Ides of March" (March 15), but he did not. On March 15, 44 B.C., his enemies stabbed him to death. They were led by Senator Cassius and Caesar's good friend, Senator Brutus.

6. Why did Brutus, Cassius, and others kill Caesar?

_____

_____

Rome Becomes an Empire (pages 440–441)

Main Idea) The Roman Republic, weakened by civil wars, became an empire under Augustus.

After Caesar was killed, another civil war broke out. Octavian, Antony, and Lepidus won the civil war. Octavian was Caesar's grandnephew. Antony and Lepidus were Caesar's best generals. In 43 B.C., they formed the Second Triumvirate.

The Second Triumvirate Soon Octavian, Antony, and Lepidus were fighting with each other. Octavian forced Lepidus to retire. Then Octavian and Antony divided the Roman world. Octavian took the west. Antony took the east.

While he was in the east, Antony fell in love with Cleopatra VII, an Egyptian queen. They made an alliance. Octavian thought they wanted Antony to be the <u>sole</u> ruler and to take over Rome, so he declared war against them.

In 31 B.C. they fought the Battle of Actium. Actium is off the west coast of Greece. Octavian crushed Antony and Cleopatra's army and navy. Antony and Cleopatra ran back to Egypt and later killed themselves.

Academic Vocabulary
sole: to be the only one in power; to be alone (p. 440)

READING ESSENTIALS AND STUDY GUIDE 9-3 (continued)

Their deaths ended Rome's period of civil wars. The Roman Republic died with them. Octavian was 32 years old when he became the ruler of the Roman world. He would lay the foundation for a different kind of government—the Roman Empire.

Who Was Augustus? Octavian knew that many people wanted to be able to vote for their leaders. Cicero agreed. He was a writer, political leader, and great speaker. Many people read Cicero's books and heard him speak. They agreed with his ideas.

Cicero supported Octavian. He thought that Octavian would rebuild the republic. In 27 B.C., Octavian said he would, but he did not. Octavian knew that the republic was too weak to solve Rome's problems. So he gave some power to the Senate, but he kept most of the power himself.

Octavian's title was *imperator,* which means "commander in chief." Soon, though, it meant "emperor." Octavian also took the title of Augustus. *Augustus* means "the revered or majestic one." After that, everyone called him Augustus.

7. How did Octavian's government reflect Cicero's ideas?

_____

_____

> **Academic Vocabulary**
>
> **foundation:** the beginning of a system or building; the first layer (p. 441)

READING ESSENTIALS AND STUDY GUIDE 9-4

The Early Empire *For use with pages 444–451*

Content Vocabulary

Pax Romana: "Roman Peace" (page 445)

aqueduct: a human-made channel that carries water long distances (page 448)

currency: money system (page 450)

Drawing From Experience

Have you ever tried to ride your bike on a dirt road or on the grass? It's a lot easier to ride on a sidewalk or a paved road.

In the previous section, you learned about Julius Caesar and Augustus and why the Roman Republic ended. In this section you will learn how Rome's good roads, water systems, and common money made the empire rich.

WH6.7 Students analyze the geographic, political, economic, religious, and social structures during the development of Rome.

Focuses on:

WH6.7.3, WH6.7.4

Organizing Your Thoughts

Augustus and other Roman emperors made many changes. Use the reading to help you list four changes and their effects.

1. _____
   _____
   _____

2. _____
   _____
   _____

3. _____
   _____
   _____

4. _____
   _____
   _____

READING ESSENTIALS AND STUDY GUIDE 9-4 (continued)

The Emperor Augustus *(pages 445–446)*

Main Idea By expanding the empire and reorganizing the military and government, Augustus created a new era of prosperity.

There had been fighting in the Mediterranean Sea area for hundreds of years. Augustus (formerly called Octavian) ended the fighting. He and his <u>successors</u> took control of the whole area. That brought *Pax Romana,* or "Roman Peace." This peace lasted 200 years.

Academic Vocabulary
successor: the person next in line as leader (p. 445)

What Did Augustus Achieve?

Augustus became emperor in 27 B.C. He decided to make the empire strong and safe. He made a professional army of about 150,000 men. All of them were Roman citizens. Augustus also made the Praetorian Guard, which had about 9,000 men. These men were specially picked to guard the emperor. Later the Praetorian Guard had a lot of political power.

Augustus's armies took Spain and Gaul (France). They also took land where Austria, Hungary, Romania, and Bulgaria are today. At the same time, Augustus built beautiful buildings and supported the arts like music, sculpture, and writing.

Augustus also bought grain from Africa for the poor. He knew that well-fed people do not rebel as much as hungry people.

At that time, more than 50 million people lived in the Roman Empire. The Empire was divided into provinces. Augustus appointed a proconsul, or governor, for each province.

He changed the tax laws. By making tax collectors government workers, he stopped them from taking some of the taxes for themselves. He also made a set of laws for free men who were not citizens. This meant that Roman laws protected everyone. Many of these free men later became citizens.

Who Came After Augustus? Augustus ruled for almost 40 years. He died in A.D. 14. A relative named Tiberius had been trained to follow him. The next three emperors—Caligula, Claudius, and Nero—were also relatives. They are called the Julio-Claudian emperors.

Not all of them were good rulers. Tiberius and Claudius ruled well, but Caligula and Nero were very cruel. Caligula was also mentally ill. He had people killed, wasted a lot of money, and even made his horse a consul! Finally the Praetorian Guard killed him, and made Claudius emperor.

Nero was also cruel. He killed many people, including his mother and two wives. He finally killed himself. Legend says that Nero played his violin when the city of Rome burned in A.D. 64.

5. What did Augustus do to make the empire safer and stronger?

_____

_____

Unity and Prosperity (pages 446–451)

Main Idea Rome's system of roads, aqueducts, ports, and common currency made the empire rich and prosperous.

Academic Vocabulary
commit: to set a goal and perform the steps necessary to achieve it (p. 446)

After Nero <u>committed</u> suicide, Rome went through a period of disorder. Four different men tried to take the title of emperor. The first one was killed by his own troops. Then Otho took over, but the legions outside of Rome did not support him. Finally, Vitellius defeated Otho in battle and became emporer.

However, the troops in Palestine did not support either of these emperors. So in A.D. 69, they declared that a general named Vespasian was emperor.

Vespasian restored peace. He began building the Colosseum, a huge amphitheatre in the middle of Rome. Vespasian also stopped several rebellions. In addition, in

A.D. 70, his son Titus's army defeated the Jews. The Romans destroyed the Jewish temple in Jerusalem.

After Vespasian died, his son, Titus, ruled. After Titus, Vespasian's other son, Domitian, ruled. Both of Vespasian's sons helped Rome to grow.

The Good Emperors From A.D. 96 to A.D. 180, a series of "good emperors" came to power. They were Nerva, Trajan, Hadrian, Antoninus Pius, and Marcus Aurelius. During their rule, trade grew, and people had a better life than before.

The five "good emperors" ruled wisely. They were among the most devoted and <u>capable</u> rulers in Rome's history. Trajan gave money to the poor. Hadrian made the laws easier to understand. Antoninus Pius passed laws to help orphans. All five hired thousands of people to build roads, bridges, monuments, harbors and aqueducts. An **aqueduct** is a human-made channel that carries water for long distances.

Academic Vocabulary
capable: the ability to contain or produce (p. 448)

A Unified Empire The good emperors conquered new territory for Rome. The empire was biggest when Trajan ruled. It spread from the Mediterranean to Britain and Mesopotamia.

But the empire was too big to rule well. Hadrian pulled troops out of Mesopotamia. In Europe, Hadrian pulled back, too. He set the empire's boundaries at the Rhine and the Danube Rivers. Hadrian also built Hadrian's Wall in northern Britain to stop the Picts and Scots from attacking. The Picts and Scots were warrior tribes in northern Britain.

In the A.D. 100s, the Roman Empire was one of the greatest empires in history. It had 3.5 million square miles of land. Most people spoke Latin or Greek.

The empire held together because people thought of themselves as Romans. Even if they spoke different languages, they had the same laws and rulers. They had many of the same customs, too. Soldiers and government workers carried Roman culture with them, and people learned it. In addition, the Romans gave many people the

READING ESSENTIALS AND STUDY GUIDE 9-4 (continued)

rights of being a citizen. In A.D. 212, every free man was made a Roman citizen.

A Booming Economy Agriculture was the most important part of the empire's economy. Farmers in Italy, Gaul (France), and Spain grew grapes and olives. Making wine and olive oil became big business. Farmers in Britain and Egypt grew grains.

There was industry with potters, weavers, and jewelers. Some cities became centers for making glass, bronze, and brass.

Traders came from all over the world to ports in Italy. They brought silk from China, spices from India, tin from Britain, lead from Spain, and iron from Gaul.

Roads and Money The Roman Empire had a good transportation system. This helped grow trade. During the *Pax Romana,* the empire had 50,000 miles of roads. The Roman navy kept pirates off the Mediterranean Sea. This meant that merchant ships were safer.

By 100 A.D., everyone in the empire used a common **currency,** or money. This made it easy to trade. It meant that a merchant in Greece could sell to a person in Italy or Egypt.

The Romans also made a system of weights and measures. People knew how much they were selling and buying. This made trade easier, too.

Ongoing Inequality Shopkeepers and merchants lived well during this time. So did skilled workers who made things. Rich Romans made their fortunes bigger. They lived in luxury.

However, most people in the cities and on the farms were still poor. And many other people were still enslaved.

6. Who were the "good emperors"? What did they accomplish?

_____

_____

Reading Essentials and Study Guide 10-1

Life in Ancient Rome *For use with pages 460–468*

Content Vocabulary

vault: a curved ceiling (page 461)

satire: a writing that teaches by making readers laugh at the silly things humans do (page 462)

ode: an emotional poem about life (page 462)

anatomy: the study of body structure (page 463)

Forum: an open space that served as a marketplace and town square (page 464)

gladiator: a man who fought animals and other men in public arenas (page 464)

paterfamilias: "father of the family" (page 465)

rhetoric: public speaking (page 465)

Drawing From Experience

Have you ever entered a science fair or had a piece of artwork displayed on a bulletin board?

In this section you will learn about life in Rome and how its people accomplished many things in art, science, and engineering.

Organizing Your Thoughts

The Romans copied the Greek ways of doing many things. But the Romans did not do them exactly as the Greeks did. Use the text to help you fill in what changes the Romans made.

	Greek Way	Roman Way
Sculpture	1.	2.
Building	3.	4.

WH6.7 Students analyze the geographic, political, economic, religious, and social structures during the development of Rome.

Focuses on:

WH6.7.8

WH7.1 Students analyze the causes and effects of the vast expansion and ultimate disintegration of the Roman Empire.

Focuses on:

WH7.1.1

READING ESSENTIALS AND STUDY GUIDE 10-1 (continued)

Roman Culture (pages 461–463)

Main Idea In addition to their own developments in science and engineering, the Romans borrowed many Greek ideas about art and literature.

The Romans copied the Greeks in many ways. They studied Greek statues, buildings, and ideas. But they changed what they copied.

What Was Roman Art Like? The Romans put Greek-style statues in their homes and public buildings. Roman artists did not carve perfect people as the Greeks had. They carved more realistic statues of people with wrinkles and warts.

The Romans used Greek-style porches on buildings. They built rows of columns, or colonnades. They were the first to make full use of the arch. Arches supported bridges, aqueducts, and buildings. They also used rows of arches together to make a **vault,** or curved ceiling. This <u>technique</u> allowed Romans to build domes.

The Romans were the first people to use concrete. Concrete buildings are stronger, so they can be built taller. One of the most famous is the Colosseum. The Colosseum was finished about A.D. 80. It was a huge arena that could seat about 60,000 people.

Another famous building is the Pantheon, a temple built for Rome's gods. The Pantheon's domed roof was the largest of its time.

Roman Literature Roman authors based much of their writing on Greek works. For example, the Roman writer Virgil got some of his ideas from Homer's *Odyssey*. Virgil wrote the epic poem called the *Aeneid*. This tells the adventures of the Trojan prince Aeneas.

The poet Horace wrote **satires** and **odes.** Satires make fun of human weaknesses. Odes are poems that express strong emotions about life. Ovid wrote stories that were based on Greek myths. The poet Catullus wrote short poems about emotions like love, sadness, and envy.

Academic Vocabulary
technique: a method used to accomplish a task (p. 461)

READING ESSENTIALS AND STUDY GUIDE 10-1 (continued)

A Roman historian named Livy wrote the *History of Rome* about 10 B.C. Livy admired Romans and thought that history could teach us moral lessons. Taking a different view, the Roman historian Tacitus thought that Rome's emperors had taken people's freedoms. He thought Romans were becoming weak.

The Romans liked plays, too. Many plays were based on Greek tragedies and comedies. Seneca wrote tragedies. Plautus and Terence wrote comedies.

Roman plays, histories, and stories were written in Latin, the main language in all of Europe. People used it for government, trade, and learning until about A.D. 1500. Latin became the foundation for many modern European languages. Many English words have Latin origins.

Roman Science and Engineering The Romans also learned from Greek science. A Greek doctor named Galen brought many medical ideas to Rome. For example, he taught them about **anatomy.** Anatomy is the study of a human or animal body.

Galen used to cut open dead animals to study how their hearts and other organs worked. He wrote and drew pictures of what he saw. Doctors studied Galen's books and drawings for more than 1,500 years.

Another important scientist was Ptolemy. He lived in Alexandria, Egypt. He mapped over 1,000 different stars. He also studied the motion of planets and stars. Ptolemy thought that Earth was the center of the universe. He was wrong about that, but he was right about many other things. People in Europe used his ideas for hundreds of years.

Roman engineers built a huge system of roads to every part of the empire. That is what people mean when they say, "All roads lead to Rome."

The Romans also built aqueducts. Aqueducts are long stone troughs that carry water. The aqueducts carried fresh water from the hills into the cities. Roman cities also had sewers to remove waste.

READING ESSENTIALS AND STUDY GUIDE 10-1 (continued)

5. Why was Roman literature written in Latin?

_____

_____

Daily Life in Rome *(pages 464–468)*

Main Idea The rich and poor had very different lives in Rome, as did men and women.

The city of Rome was laid out in a square with the **Forum** in the middle. The Forum was an open space that served as a marketplace and public square. Temples and public buildings sat around it.

Rich Romans lived in large houses. Each home had big rooms, fine furniture, and gardens. In the center of each house was an inner court called an atrium. Rich Romans also had homes called villas on their country estates.

Most people in Rome were poor. They lived in apartment buildings made of stone and wood. Rents were high. Whole families lived in one room.

Roman apartment buildings could be six stories high. They were not well built. The people who lived in them used torches and lamps, so there was a <u>constant</u> threat of fires.

This part of Rome was crowded and dirty. People threw trash into the streets. There were many thieves. The Roman government did some things to keep people from rioting. The government gave the poor "bread and circuses." This means that the poor got some free food and shows.

Some of the shows were chariot races and gladiator contests. **Gladiators** fought animals and each other. Most gladiators were enslaved people, criminals, or poor people.

What Was Family Life Like? Roman families included parents, young children, married children, their families, other relatives, and enslaved servants. The father was called

Academic Vocabulary
constant: occurring over and over again (p. 464)

the **paterfamilias.** That means "father of the family." He controlled the other family members.

Rich Romans hired tutors to teach their children. Some older boys from rich families went away to learn reading, writing, and **rhetoric.** *Rhetoric* means "public speaking." Girls studied reading and writing at home. They also learned household duties. Poor people did not go to school.

Roman boys "came of age" when they were between 14 and 16. To celebrate, they burned their toys. This showed that they were no longer boys. They could become soldiers or join the government. Many became partners in family businesses. Men wore togas, which are loose robes.

Roman women did not become adults until they married. Women wore long flowing robes with cloaks. The cloaks were called *palla.*

Women in Rome Women in early Rome had some rights but were not full citizens. They could not vote.

Rich women had a lot of freedom. They could own land, run businesses, and sell property. They could go to the theater or Colosseum. Enslaved people did the housework. This gave rich women time to study literature, art, and fashion.

Women with less money worked in their homes or in family businesses. They were allowed to leave home to shop, visit friends, worship at temples, or go to the baths. Some women did work independently outside the home. Some were priestesses. Others were hairdressers or doctors.

How Did Romans Treat Enslaved People? Slavery was always a part of the Roman Empire. But as the empire grew, more and more people were enslaved. By 100 B.C., about 40 percent of the people in Italy were enslaved.

Enslaved people worked in homes, fields, mines, and workshops. They helped build roads, bridges, and aqueducts. Many enslaved Greeks were well educated. They were teachers, doctors, and artisans.

READING ESSENTIALS AND STUDY GUIDE 10-1 (continued)

For most enslaved people, life was hard. They often rebelled. In 73 B.C. a gladiator named Spartacus led 70,000 enslaved people against Rome. They beat several Roman armies. Rome finally conquered them two years later. Spartacus and 6,000 others were killed.

Roman Religion and Philosophy The ancient Romans worshiped many gods and goddesses. They believed that spirits lived in things like trees and rivers. Roman emperors also were worshiped.

The Romans adopted Greek gods and goddesses. They gave them Roman names. For example, the Greek god Zeus became the Roman god Jupiter, the sky god.

Romans offered food and prayer to their gods and goddesses. The important gods and goddesses of Rome were honored in the temples. In addition, every Roman home had an altar for household gods.

Some Roman priests looked for messages from the gods. They studied the insides of dead animals and watched the way that birds flew.

When the Romans conquered other people, they let them keep their religion, as long as the religion did not threaten the empire.

6. Describe the freedoms of upper-class women that were not available to women of other classes.

_____

_____

READING ESSENTIALS AND STUDY GUIDE 10-2

The Fall of Rome *For use with pages 474–483*

Content Vocabulary

inflation: prices that rise quickly (page 476)

barter: to exchange goods and services without using money (page 476)

reform: political change to make things better (page 477)

Drawing From Experience

Think about why sports teams sometimes lose games. Someone might not be able to play. The other team might be better. People make silly mistakes. Most of the time there are a couple of reasons that a team loses.

In the previous section, you learned about life in Rome and how its people accomplished many things in art, science, and engineering. In this section, you will learn about the problems Rome experienced and why the Roman Empire fell.

Organizing Your Thoughts

Many things led to the fall of the Roman Empire. Use the reading to help you fill in the boxes with reasons that the empire fell.

WH6.7 Students analyze the geographic, political, economic, religious, and social structures during the development of Rome.

Focuses on:

WH6.7.7, WH6.7.8

WH7.1 Students analyze the causes and effects of the vast expansion and ultimate disintegration of the Roman Empire.

Focuses on:

WH7.1.1, WH7.1.2

1. _____ + 2. _____ + 3. _____ +

4. _____ + 5. _____ = **Fall of the Roman Empire**

The Decline of Rome (pages 475–477)

Main Idea Poor leadership, a declining economy, and attacks by Germanic tribes weakened the Roman Empire.

Marcus Aurelius died in A.D. 180. He was the last of the "good emperors." His son, Commodus, became emperor. Commodus was cruel and wasted money. In A.D. 192 the emperor's bodyguard killed him.

After Commodus, a new group of emperors ruled Rome. They were named the Severans. People rebelled many times while the Severans were rulers. The Severans paid the army well, so they stayed in power. But the Severans did not deal with the reasons why people were rebelling. They ignored the empire's growing crime and poverty.

Political and Social Problems The last Severan ruler died in A.D. 235. Army leaders fought constantly for the throne. In 50 years, Rome had 22 different emperors.

Rome had many other problems. Government officials took bribes. Many wealthy citizens stopped paying taxes. Fewer people went to school, and a large number were enslaved. Wealthy Romans supported slavery because it was a cheap way to get work done.

Economic and Military Problems Rome's economy began to fall apart. Law and order broke down. Roman soldiers and invaders seized crops. They destroyed fields. Farmers grew less food. People went hungry.

People bought fewer things. Artisans made less. Shopkeepers lost money. Businesses closed, and people lost their jobs. Many workers had to leave jobs and serve in the army.

Rome also faced **inflation.** During inflation, prices go up very quickly. Money loses its value. How does money lose its value? As you just read, the rich were not paying taxes. The bad economy meant that other people had no money to pay taxes. So, the government had less tax

READING ESSENTIALS AND STUDY GUIDE 10-2 (continued)

money to spend. But the government still needed to pay for things. It needed to pay soldiers and the people who built things.

The government started making coins with less gold in them. But people soon learned that the coins did not have as much gold in them. The coins began losing value. Prices went up, and many people stopped using money. They **bartered** for things. Barter means to trade goods without using money.

Then Germanic tribes raided the western empire. Persian armies attacked the eastern empire. Soon the government did not have enough soldiers. The Roman government tried using Germanic warriors, but they were not loyal to Rome.

What Were Diocletian's Reforms? In A.D. 284 General Diocletian became emperor. He made **reforms** to stop the empire's decline, or fall. Reforms are political changes to make things better.

Diocletian divided the empire into four parts. He named officials to rule these areas, but he kept <u>authority</u> over all four sections. He also tried to fix the economy. He set the prices of goods. He set wages. He also told workers to keep the same jobs until they died.

Diocletian's reforms failed. People ignored his rules, and he could not make them obey.

Academic Vocabulary
authority: the right to give commands (p. 477)

Who Was Constantine? Diocletian retired in A.D. 305. Seven years later, General **Constantine** became emperor. Constantine made some new rules to help the economy. He said that the sons of workers had to do what their fathers did. The sons of farmers had to farm the same land their fathers worked. The sons of soldiers had to serve in the army.

Constantine's changes did not stop the empire's decline in the west. So Constantine moved the capital away from Rome. He moved the capital east, to the old

READING ESSENTIALS AND STUDY GUIDE 10-2 (continued)

city of Byzantium. He rebuilt the city and called it Constantinople. Today, Constantinople is called Istanbul.

6. How did Diocletian try to reverse the decline of Rome?

_____

_____

Rome Falls (pages 479–481)

Main Idea Rome finally fell when invaders swept through the empire during the A.D. 400s.

Constantine died in A.D. 337. Fighting broke out again. Theodosius finally gained control and ended the fighting. He decided that the empire should be split into two. When he died in A.D. 395, it was split into the Western Roman Empire with its capital at Rome and the Eastern Roman Empire with its capital at Constantinople.

Rome Is Invaded As Rome declined, it could not keep out the Germanic tribes. There were many Germanic groups—Ostrogoths, Visigoths, Franks, Vandals, Angles, and Saxons. They came from northern Europe.

These tribes wanted warmer climates and better land for their cattle. They also liked Rome's wealth and culture. In addition, they were fleeing the Huns, warriors from Asia.

In the late A.D. 300s, the Huns entered Eastern Europe. They beat the Ostrogoths. The Visigoths asked the Eastern Roman emperor for protection. He let them settle just inside the empire's border. In return they promised to be loyal to Rome.

Soon, though, the Visigoths and Romans started fighting. The empire made the Visigoths pay very high prices for food. The Romans also enslaved many Visigoths.

The Visigoths rebelled. In A.D. 378 they defeated Roman legions at the Battle of Adrianople. Rome had to give land to the Visigoths.

More and more Germanic warriors came into the Roman Empire for land. In the winter of A.D. 406, the Rhine River in Western Europe froze. Germanic groups crossed the frozen river into Gaul (today's France). The Romans were too weak to keep them out.

In A.D. 410, the Visigoths captured Rome. They were led by **Alaric.** It was the first time Rome had been conquered in 800 years.

The Vandals—another Germanic group—overran Spain and northern Africa. They enslaved some Roman landowners. They drove others away. Then the Vandals sailed to Italy. In A.D. 455 they entered Rome. They stole and burned Rome for 12 days. The English word *vandalism* comes from these attacks. *Vandalism* means "the willful destruction of property."

Rome Falls By the mid-A.D. 400s, several Germanic leaders held high posts in Rome's government and army. In A.D. 476 a Germanic general named Odoacer threw out the western emperor. The emperor was a 14-year-old boy named Romulus Augustulus. Romulus Augustulus was the last emperor to rule from Rome. Historians say that this event was the end of the Western Roman Empire.

Odoacer controlled Rome for almost 15 years. Then a group of Visigoths took over. They killed Odoacer. They set up a kingdom in Italy under their leader, Theodoric. Other Germanic tribes set up kingdoms in Europe, too.

By A.D. 550, the Western Roman Empire was gone. But people still did things in Roman ways. For example, Germanic rulers spoke and wrote in Latin. They used Roman laws. They were also Christians.

READING ESSENTIALS AND STUDY GUIDE 10-2 (continued)

The Western Roman Empire had fallen. But the Eastern Roman Empire prospered. It became known as the Byzantine Empire and lasted nearly 1,000 more years.

7. Which event usually marks the fall of the Western Roman Empire?

_____

_____

The Legacy of Rome *(pages 482–483)*

Main Idea Rome passed on many achievements in government, law, language, and the arts.

Our world would be very different if the Roman Empire had never existed. Many words in the English language come from the Romans. Many of our ideas about government, laws, and building come from the Romans, too. As you will read in the next chapter, Roman rule led to peace and order. This let the Christian religion spread.

Roman Ideas and Government Today As you read earlier, the Romans first wrote their laws on the Twelve Tables. We still use those ideas today. For example, we believe that all people are equal under the law. We expect our judges to be fair. We think that people are innocent until they are proven guilty.

We use Roman ideas about government and citizenship, too. The U.S. is a republic made up of equal citizens. We think that that is the best form of government. We also think that people should vote and do their duty. We think that people should try to make society better.

READING ESSENTIALS AND STUDY GUIDE 10-2 (continued)

Roman Influence on Culture Today, we use the <u>expanded</u> Latin alphabet in most of the Western world. Many modern languages—Italian, Spanish, French—come from Latin. Many English words come from Latin, too. Scientists, doctors, and lawyers still use Latin phrases. Plants and animals have Latin names.

Academic Vocabulary
expand: to increase in number, size, or amount (p. 483)

We also use many Roman ideas about building. Many modern buildings use concrete. Roman architectural styles are still popular, too. Many buildings—especially churches and city and state buildings—have domes and arches. Those were copied from Roman buildings.

Christianity As you probably know, Christianity is a major religion today. Christianity began in the Roman Empire. Rome's government adopted Christianity in the A.D. 300s. It helped the new religion to grow and spread.

8. Name some things from the Roman Empire that we still use today.

_____

_____

READING ESSENTIALS AND STUDY GUIDE 10-3

The Byzantine Empire *For use with pages 484–491*

Content Vocabulary

mosaic: picture made from bits of colored glass and stone (page 490)

saint: Christian holy person (page 490)

regent: a person who acts as a ruler when the real ruler is too young or sick (page 491)

Drawing From Experience

Think about your school and town. Are there people from different cultures? Do these people share different types of food, stories, and holidays with your community?

Constantinople had people from many different cultures, too. In the previous section, you learned the reasons the Roman Empire fell. In this section you will learn about Constantinople and the Byzantine Empire. You will also learn about Emperor Justinian.

WH7.1 Students analyze the causes and effects of the vast expansion and ultimate disintegration of the Roman Empire.

Focuses on:

WH7.1.3

Organizing Your Thoughts

Constantinople was one of the greatest cities in the world. Use the text to help you name three reasons that Constantinople grew rich and strong.

1.	_____
2.	_____
3.	_____

The Rise of the Byzantines (pages 485–486)

Main Idea The Eastern Roman Empire grew rich and powerful as the Western Roman Empire fell.

The Eastern Roman Empire was called the Byzantine Empire. In the A.D. 500s the empire stretched west to Italy, south to Egypt, and east to Arabia. Many of the people in the empire were Greeks, but Egyptians, Syrians, Arabs, Armenians, Jews, Persians, Slavs, and Turks lived in the empire, too.

Why Is Constantinople Important? You already learned that Constantine moved the capital of the Roman Empire to Constantinople. After the western empire fell, Constantinople became the capital of the Byzantine Empire. By the A.D. 500s, Constantinople was one of the world's great cities.

One reason for Constantinople's success was its location. It had good harbors near the Black Sea and the Aegean Sea. Constantinople was also a major stop on the trade routes between Europe and Asia. The trade routes made the city rich.

Constantinople was also easy to protect. It was on a peninsula. Seas protected it on three sides. A huge wall guarded the city on the fourth side.

Influence of Greek Culture At first, some Byzantines kept Roman ways. Constantinople was known as the "New Rome." Its public buildings and palaces were built in the Roman style. The city even had an oval arena called the Hippodrome. Chariot races and other events were held there.

Emperors spoke Latin and enforced Roman laws. The empire's poor people received free bread and shows. Wealthy people lived in town or on large farming estates. Many of them had lived in Rome.

But many other people spoke Greek and had Greek habits. Soon Byzantine rulers began to speak Greek. The Byzantines also copied ideas from the Egyptians, the

Slavs, and the Persians. All of these cultures blended together. This led to new ideas in learning and the arts. Between A.D. 500 and A.D. 1200, the Byzantines had one of the world's greatest empires.

4. What cultures blended together in the Byzantine Empire?

_____

_____

Emperor Justinian *(pages 486–487)*

Main Idea The policies and reforms of Emperor Justinian and Empress Theodora helped make the Byzantine Empire strong.

Justinian became emperor of the Byzantine Empire in A.D. 527. He ruled until A.D. 565. Justinian was a strong leader. He controlled the military, made laws, and was supreme judge. His order could not be questioned.

Justinian's wife was the empress Theodora. She helped Justinian make decisions and choose government officials.

Theodora was a former actress. She was intelligent and strong-willed. Theodora convinced Justinian that women should have some rights. For the first time, a Byzantine wife could own land. That way, if she became a widow, she had <u>income</u> to take care of her children.

In A.D. 532 Theodora helped save Justinian's throne. Angry taxpayers threatened to overthrow Justinian. They stormed the palace. Justinian's advisors urged him to leave the city. Theodora told him to stay and fight. Justinian stayed and crushed the uprising.

Justinian's Conquests Justinian wanted to reunite the Roman Empire. To do this, he had to conquer Western Europe and northern Africa. He ordered General Belisarius to lead the Byzantine army.

Belisarius added a lot of cavalry to the army. Instead of foot soldiers, the army came to <u>rely</u> on cavalry—soldiers

Academic Vocabulary

income: pay received from work done (p. 487)

Academic Vocabulary

rely: to depend on (p. 487)

READING ESSENTIALS AND STUDY GUIDE 10-3 (continued)

on horses. Byzantine cavalry wore armor. They carried bows and lances, which were long spears.

Justinian's army conquered most of Italy and northern Africa. It also beat the Persians in the east. But it was done too quickly. When Justinian died, the empire could not keep all of the land in the west.

Justinian's Law Code Justinian thought that the empire's laws were too difficult to understand. He put together a group of legal scholars headed by Tribonian. He ordered the scholars to reform the law code.

The new code became known as the Justinian Code. Common people could understand the empire's new laws. The Justinian Code influenced the laws of almost every country in Europe.

5. What did Justinian accomplish during his reign?

_____

_____

Byzantine Civilization (pages 489–491)

Main Idea The Byzantines developed a rich culture based on Roman, Greek, and Christian ideas.

From the A.D. 500s to the A.D. 1100s, the Byzantine Empire was the center of trade between Europe and Asia. There were trade goods from present-day Russia, the Mediterranean, Europe in the west, and Persia and China in the east. People traded spices, gems, metals, cloth, farm goods, furs, honey, and enslaved people.

This <u>enormous</u> trade made the Byzantine Empire very rich. However, most Byzantines were not merchants. Most people were farmers, herders, laborers, or artisans. A major Byzantine industry was weaving silk. It developed around A.D. 550. It started when Byzantine travelers smuggled silkworm eggs out of China. They raised the silkworms. The silkworms made silk threads. Weavers used the threads to make silk cloth.

Academic Vocabulary
enormous: great in size or number (p. 489)

READING ESSENTIALS AND STUDY GUIDE 10-3 (continued)

Byzantine Art and Architecture The Byzantine Empire lasted about 1,000 years. Constantinople was the largest and richest city in Europe. The Byzantines were educated and creative. They shared Greek and Roman ideas with other cultures. They invented new types of art.

Justinian and other Byzantine emperors had many churches, forts, and public buildings built. Constantinople alone had hundreds of churches and palaces. One of Justinian's greatest achievements was building the huge church called Hagia Sophia. *Hagia Sophia* means "Holy Wisdom." It was completed in A.D. 537. It was the religious center of the Byzantine Empire. It still stands today in Istanbul.

The walls of Hagia Sophia are lined with beautiful marble and mosaics. **Mosaics** are pictures made from many bits of colored glass or stone. They were an important type of Byzantine art. Mosaics often showed **saints,** or Christian holy people.

Byzantine Women The family was the center of social life. Religion and the government said that marriage and family life were important. It was hard to get a divorce.

Most Byzantine women did not lead independent lives. They had to stay home and take care of their families. However, women did gain some important rights, thanks to Empress Theodora. Some Byzantine women became well educated. They got involved in politics. Several royal women served as regents. A **regent** is a person who stands in for a ruler who is too young or too ill to govern. A few ruled the empire on their own.

Byzantine Education Learning was highly respected. Boys studied religion, medicine, law, arithmetic, grammar, and other subjects. Wealthy Byzantines sometimes hired tutors to teach their children. Girls usually were taught at home.

Most Byzantine authors wrote about religion. They said that people needed to obey God. They wrote about the lives of saints. Byzantine writers also copied and

READING ESSENTIALS AND STUDY GUIDE 10-3 (continued)

shared ancient Greek and Roman writings. Without Byzantine copies, we would not have many important works from the ancient world.

6. Which church is one of Justinian's greatest achievements?

_____

_____

READING ESSENTIALS AND STUDY GUIDE 11-1

The First Christians *For use with pages 500–508*

Content Vocabulary

messiah: a savior or someone who rescues another from harm (page 502)

disciple: a person who follows the teachings of another (page 502)

parable: a story that teaches a lesson using everyday events (page 503)

resurrection: act of rising from the dead or coming back to life (page 505)

apostle: one of the early Christian leaders who had been chosen by Jesus to spread his message (page 506)

salvation: being delivered or saved from sin, destruction, or evil (page 508)

Drawing from Experience

Have you ever been forced to do something that you did not want to do? Did you fight back, or did you go along with the rules?

In this section, you will learn how some Jews opposed the Roman rule of Judaea peacefully, while others fought back. You'll also learn how Jesus' teachings brought about a new religion called Christianity.

WH6.7 Students analyze the geographic, political, economic, religious, and social structures during the development of Rome.

Focuses on:

WH6.7.5, WH6.7.6, WH6.7.7

Organizing Your Thoughts

Use the diagram to help you take notes on some of the first Christians.

People	What did they do? (cause)	What happened? (effect)
King David & King Solomon	1.	2.
Zealots	3.	4.
Jesus	5.	6.
Peter	7.	8.
Paul	9.	10.

The Jews and the Romans *(page 501)*

Main Idea Roman rule of Judaea led some Jews to oppose Rome peacefully, while others rebelled.

During the 900s B.C., King David and King Solomon brought the Israelites together to create the kingdom of Israel. Jerusalem became the capital. This unity did not last long and was split into two smaller kingdoms: Israel and Judah. These did not last long either, and the kingdoms were taken over by more powerful neighbors. Israel was ruined, and its people went in different directions. The people of Judah, called the Jews, survived.

Roman Rule The Romans took over Judah in 63 B.C. For a time, Judah was ruled by Jewish kings. Then, in A.D. 6, Emperor Augustus changed the country's name to Judaea. He made Judaea a Roman province or territory. It was ruled by a Roman governor called a procurator instead of a king.

The Jews were divided over what to do about the Romans. Some wanted to work with the Romans, but others did not. Some rebelled by closely following their Jewish traditions. Others rejected the Romans and moved away to places where they could live by themselves and share their belongings.

The Jews Rebel Some Jews, called Zealots, wanted to fight the Romans and get their kingdom back. In A.D. 66, the Zealots fought with many Jews against the Romans, but they lost. The Romans destroyed the temple and killed thousands of Jews. The Jewish general Josephus wrote about how horrible the war was. He had fought in the war, but changed to the Roman side.

In A.D. 132, the Jews fought against the Romans again and lost again. This time the Romans forced all Jews to leave Jerusalem and would not let them return to the city. Many Jews were very sad they lost Jerusalem. They found homes in other places.

By A.D. 700, Jewish communities were set up as far west as Spain and as far east as central Asia. In later centuries, they formed communities throughout Europe and the Americas. Even though they were not all living in one location, they kept their faith alive by studying and following their religious laws.

11. How many wars did the Jews fight against the Romans? Did they win any of them?

_____

_____

The Life of Jesus *(pages 502–505)*

Main Idea Jesus of Nazareth preached of God's love and forgiveness. According to Christian scriptures, Jesus was crucified and rose from the dead.

During Roman times, many Jews hoped that God would send them a **messiah,** or a leader who would rescue them from the Romans and help them win back their freedom. Long ago, Israelites predicted that a messiah would come. Many Jews thought this messiah would be a great king and would give them back their kingdom.

A few <u>decades</u> before the first Jewish fight against the Romans, a Jew named Jesus left his home in Nazareth and began preaching. From about A.D. 30 to A.D. 33, Jesus went throughout Judaea and Galilee to the north and taught his ideas. Crowds would come to hear him teach and soon he had 12 close followers called **disciples.**

What Did Jesus Teach? According to the Christian Bible, Jesus taught that following Jewish religious laws was not as important as having a relationship with God. Jesus said that God was his Father. He preached that God was coming soon to rule the world. He asked people to turn from their sins.

Academic Vocabulary
decade: a period of ten years (p. 502)

Jesus' Sermon on the Mount gives the main points of his teachings. He taught that God wanted more than people who just followed religious laws. He wanted people to love and forgive from the heart. "Blessed are the merciful, for they will obtain mercy" and "Blessed are the peacemakers, for they will be called children of God" are two of Jesus' sayings.

Jesus taught about love and forgiveness because he said God loves and forgives people. He said that God's command is simple. He repeated the age-old Jewish teaching: "Love the Lord your God with all your heart and with all your soul and with all your mind and with all your strength." Jesus also stressed another Jewish teaching: "Love your neighbor as yourself." This message of love and forgiveness helped shape the values many people in Europe and America hold today.

Jesus used stories to teach a lesson. These are called **parables.** He used everyday events to teach spiritual ideas. In the story of the prodigal (wasteful) son, Jesus told how a father welcomed back his son with open arms. He forgave his son's mistakes. In another story, he told how a shepherd left his entire flock of sheep to go find one lost sheep. Both stories taught that God forgives mistakes and wants all people to turn away from bad deeds to be saved.

One of the best-known parables is about the Good Samaritan. This story is about a man who is beaten by robbers. A priest and another religious leader pass by the injured man, but a Samaritan, a member of a group who lived in what is now northern Israel, stops to help the man. He cleans his cuts and pays for his stay at an inn (hotel). Jesus asked his followers, "Which man do you think truly showed love to his neighbor?"

What Is the Crucifixion? People had strong responses to Jesus and his message. Many said he healed the sick and did other miracles. They said he was the messiah. Other Jews

READING ESSENTIALS AND STUDY GUIDE 11-1 (continued)

did not agree and said he was tricking them. The Roman rulers were scared of what might happen because of Jesus' teachings. They thought a person who could get such strong reactions might threaten law and order.

To celebrate an important Jewish holiday, Passover, Jesus went to Jerusalem in about A.D. 33. Large, cheering crowds met him. In an event known as the Last Supper, Jesus celebrated the holiday with his 12 disciples. The leaders in Jerusalem feared trouble, so they arrested Jesus. He was charged with not being loyal to the government. According to Christian scriptures, he was punished by being crucified, or hung from a cross until dead. This was Rome's way of punishing lower-class criminals and people who spoke up against the government.

After Jesus' death, his followers made a surprising claim. They said that Jesus had been **resurrected,** or raised from the dead. Christian tradition states that Mary Magdalene, one of Jesus' followers, was the first to see Jesus alive again. Others, including Jesus' disciples, reported seeing him as well. The disciples said that Jesus' empty tomb was proof that he was the messiah. All of this led to a new religion called Christianity.

12. What is a parable? Give one example that Jesus used.

_____

_____

The First Christians (pages 506–508)

Main Idea) Jesus' life and a belief in his resurrection led to a new religion called Christianity.

Jesus' disciples spread the news about his teachings and resurrection. Small groups in the Greek-speaking cities of the eastern Mediterranean agreed with this message. Some were Jews, but others were not. People who

believed Jesus and his teachings became known
as Christians. They called him Jesus Christ. The word
Christ comes from *Christos*, a Greek word for "messiah."

The early Christians built churches for worship and
teaching. They met in people's houses. Many of these
homes were owned by women. In these meetings, Christians prayed and studied the Hebrew Bible. They also
shared in a meal like the Last Supper to remember Jesus'
death and resurrection.

Who Were Peter and Paul? Christian leaders who were chosen
by Jesus to spread his message were called **apostles.** They
helped to spread Christianity. Perhaps the two most
important apostles were Peter and Paul.

Simon Peter was a Jewish fisherman. When Jesus was
alive, Peter knew him and was one of the 12 people Jesus
called to preach his message. Christian tradition says that
after Jesus died, Peter went to Rome and helped set up a
church there. Today, the leader of Catholic Christians
<u>resides</u> in Rome.

Paul of Tarsus was another important Christian leader.
He was a well-educated Jew and a Roman citizen. At first,
Paul worked to stop Christian ideas from spreading. The
head Jewish priest in Jerusalem sent him to a city in Syria
called Damascus. The priest wanted Paul to stop Christians in Damascus from spreading their ideas.

On his way to Damascus, something strange happened
to Paul. According to Christian belief, he saw a great light
and heard Jesus' voice. Paul became a Christian and spent
the rest of his life spreading Jesus' message. He traveled
a lot and started many churches throughout the eastern
Mediterranean.

What Do Christians Believe? Christians taught that Jesus was the
Son of God and had come to save people. By accepting
Jesus and his teachings, people could gain **salvation.** This
means they could be saved from sin and allowed to enter

Academic Vocabulary
reside: to live in a particular place (p. 506)

heaven. Like Jesus, after death they would be raised to live with God forever.

Because of their faith in Jesus, Christians began to understand God in a new way. Like the Jews, Christians believed in the God of Israel. They studied the Hebrew Bible. But most Christians believed that the one God was three persons: Father, Son, and Holy Spirit. This idea became known as the Trinity, which means "three."

13. If someone was known as a Christian, what did that person believe in?

_____

_____

READING ESSENTIALS AND STUDY GUIDE 11-2

The Christian Church *For use with pages 509–514*

Content Vocabulary

persecute: to treat someone badly (page 511)

martyr: someone who is willing to die instead of giving up their beliefs (page 511)

hierarchy: a group of people with different levels of power or authority (page 513)

clergy: leaders of the church (page 513)

laity: regular church members (page 513)

doctrine: official church teaching (page 513)

gospel: one of the first four books of the New Testament: Matthew, Mark, Luke, and John (page 513)

pope: head of the Catholic church and bishop of Rome (page 514)

Drawing From Experience

Have you ever joined a group or a club? What did you like and dislike about it?

The last section described how Jesus' teachings led to a new religion called Christianity. This section discusses how the Roman Empire made Christianity its official religion and how early churches developed.

Organizing Your Thoughts

Use the diagram to help you take notes. List the reasons why Christianity attracted so many people.

WH6.7 Students analyze the geographic, political, economic, religious, and social structures during the development of Rome.

Focuses on:

WH6.7.7

WH7.1 Students analyze the causes and effects of the vast expansion and ultimate disintegration of the Roman Empire.

Focuses on:

WH7.1.3

Why did Christianity attract so many people?

1.

2.

3.

READING ESSENTIALS AND STUDY GUIDE 11-2 (continued)

A Growing Faith (pages 510–512)

Main Idea Christianity won many followers and eventually became the official religion of the Roman Empire.

During the 100 years after Jesus' death, many people throughout the Roman world began to follow Christianity. The Roman Empire helped spread Christian ideas. Christians used Roman roads to carry their message from place to place. The peace and order <u>established</u> by Rome made it safe to travel. Since most of the empire's people spoke either Latin or Greek, Christians could talk with them directly.

Why did so many people follow Christianity? First, the Christian teachings gave meaning to people's lives. Rome's religion told people to honor the government. Christianity gave hope and comfort to the poor and powerless instead.

Second, the ideas of Christianity were like ideas from other religions already known by the Romans. These religions also appealed to people's emotions and promised happiness after death.

Finally, Christianity gave people the chance to be part of a caring group. Within their churches, Christians worshiped together and helped each other. They took care of the sick, older people, wives who had lost their husbands, and children without parents. Many women could take on new jobs in Christianity. They ran churches from their homes, spread Jesus' message, and helped care for people in need.

How Did the Romans Treat Christians? Over time, the Roman government began to see Christians as a threat. Romans believed everyone should honor the emperor as a god. Christians, like the Jews, would not do this. They believed that only God could be worshiped. They also would not serve in the army or hold public positions. They talked

Academic Vocabulary
establish: to put securely in place (p. 510)

READING ESSENTIALS AND STUDY GUIDE 11-2 (continued)

badly about Roman festivals and games. Because of this, the Romans felt that Christians were not loyal. The government began to punish them.

In A.D. 64, the Roman government began to treat badly or **persecute** Christians. The emperor Nero blamed Christians for starting a fire that burned much of Rome. Christianity was made illegal, and many Christians were killed.

During these hard times, many Christians became **martyrs.** This means they chose to die instead of give up their beliefs. Romans required the dead to be cremated, or burned to ashes. Christians wanted to bury their dead. In Rome, Christians were forced to bury their dead in underground burial places, or catacombs.

Rome Adopts Christianity Even with all the bad things that were happening, Christianity still spread. After a while, it attracted people from both lower and upper classes. After A.D. 200, many Romans grew tired of war and were scared the empire would fall apart. They began to admire the faith and courage of the Christians. At the same time, many Christians started to accept the empire.

In the early A.D. 300s, the emperor Diocletian persecuted many Christians. But he could not stop Christianity. The Roman government realized that Christianity was too strong to be ended by force.

Then, in A.D. 312, the Roman emperor Constantine accepted Christianity. According to tradition, Constantine saw a flaming cross in the sky as he was about to go into battle. Written beneath the cross were the Latin words "In this sign you will conquer." Constantine won the battle and believed that the Christian God had helped him.

In A.D. 313, Constantine <u>issued</u> an order called the Edict of Milan. This meant that people could practice whatever religion they wanted. This made Christianity legal. Constantine's government supported Christianity. With the help of his mother, Helena, he built churches in Rome and Jerusalem. He also let church leaders have government jobs and did not make them pay taxes.

Academic Vocabulary
issue: to distribute officially (p. 512)

READING ESSENTIALS AND STUDY GUIDE 11-2 (continued)

The emperor after Constantine, Theodosius I, made Christianity Rome's official religion in A.D. 392. At the same time, he made all other religions illegal.

4. Why did the Romans feel that Christians should be punished?

_____

_____

The Early Church (*pages 513–514*)

Main Idea) **Early Christians set up a church organization and explained their beliefs.**

In its early years, Christianity was not well organized. Leaders like Paul traveled from one Christian community to another. They tried to <u>unify</u> the different groups. They taught that all the separate groups of Christians were part of one body called the church. But they had a problem. How could they join together as one?

Academic Vocabulary
unify: to bring together (p. 513)

Organizing the Church The early Christians organized the church in a surprising way. They copied the Roman Empire structure that was a **hierarchy.** This is a group with different levels of power or authority.

The leaders of the church were the **clergy.** They had special jobs. The regular church members were called the **laity.** As the church grew, women were not allowed to be leaders of the church. However, as regular church members, they took care of the sick and needy.

By around A.D. 300, priests led local churches. Many churches formed a diocese, or a district, led by a bishop. Sometimes a bishop in charge of a city diocese was also put in charge of an entire region. This made him an archbishop. The five top archbishops became known as patriarchs. They led churches in large cities and were in charge of large areas of land.

The bishops explained Christian beliefs. They also were in charge of church business. Every now and then, they met to discuss questions about Christian belief. Decisions they made at these meetings became **doctrine,** or official church teaching.

What Is the New Testament? Church leaders explained Christian ideas and took special care of the writings about the life of Jesus. These writings helped guide Christians. Jesus himself did not leave any writings. Instead, his followers retold what they knew about him. By A.D. 300, four records of Jesus' life, teachings, and resurrection were well known. Christians believe these were written by early followers of Jesus named Matthew, Mark, Luke, and John.

Each of these records is called a **gospel.** *Gospel* means "good news." Christians put these four gospels together with the writings of Paul and other early Christian leaders. All of these writings form the New Testament of the Christian Bible.

Early Christians were also affected by other important writings. Church Fathers wrote books to explain church teachings. One leading Church Father was a bishop in North Africa named Augustine. In his writings, Augustine explained Christianity to people who did not believe in it. He wrote *The City of God*—one of the first history books written from a Christian viewpoint. He also wrote a book called *Confessions.* It was a story of his personal journey to Christian faith.

Who Is the Pope? As the church grew, the bishop of Rome started to claim power over the other bishops. He believed that he had the power of Peter, Jesus' leading disciple, or follower. Also, Rome was the district over which he ruled. Rome was the capital of the empire.

By A.D. 600, the bishop of Rome had gained a special name—**pope.** This name comes from a Latin word meaning "father." Latin-speaking Christians accepted the pope as head of the church. Their churches became known as the Roman Catholic Church. Greek-speaking Christians would not welcome the pope's authority or power over them. You will read in the next section about Christians in the Eastern Roman Empire. They had a different form of Christianity.

5. What are the four gospels that form the New Testament of the Christian Bible?

_____

_____

READING ESSENTIALS AND STUDY GUIDE 11-3

The Spread of Christian Ideas   *For use with pages 515–521*

Content Vocabulary

icon: picture or image of Jesus, Mary (the mother of Jesus), and the saints (Christian holy people) (page 516)

iconoclast: someone who attacks traditional beliefs or institutions (page 517)

excommunicate: to say that a person or group no longer belongs to the church (page 518)

schism: a separation or split (page 518)

monastery: a place where men called monks live together in a religious community (page 519)

missionary: person who teaches religion to those who do not believe (page 519)

Drawing From Experience

Have you ever lost a friend because each of you believed in two different things? How did that make you feel?

The last section described how Christianity became the official religion of the Roman Empire and how early churches developed. In this section, you will learn how the church was divided and how Christian ideas spread.

Organizing Your Thoughts

Use the diagram to help you take notes. List the religious conflicts that led to the split between the Roman Catholic Church and the Eastern Orthodox Church.

WH6.7 Students analyze the geographic, political, economic, religious, and social structures during the development of Rome.

Focuses on:

WH6.7.7

WH7.1 Students analyze the causes and effects of the vast expansion and ultimate disintegration of the Roman Empire.

Focuses on:

WH7.1.3

Religious Conflicts

1. _____

2. _____

3. _____

The Byzantine Church (pages 516–518)

Main Idea) Church and government worked closely together in the Byzantine Empire.

As you know, the church of Rome <u>survived</u> the fall of the Western Roman Empire. The pope became the strongest leader in Western Europe. Latin churches of the area became known as the Roman Catholic Church. In the East, however, the Roman Empire continued. It became the Byzantine Empire. Like Roman Catholics in the West, the Byzantines created their own form of Christianity. It was based on their Greek heritage and was known as the Eastern Orthodox Church.

Church and State Church and government worked closely together in the Byzantine Empire. The Byzantines believed their emperor symbolized Jesus Christ on Earth. The emperor was given a crown in a religious ceremony.

The emperor controlled the Church and the government. He chose the patriarch, or person who would rule Constantinople and lead the Church in the Byzantine Empire. Byzantines believed that God wanted them to protect and spread Christianity. All Church and government officials agreed with this goal.

Religious Arguments All Byzantines were interested in religious matters. In homes and shops, they argued about religious questions. For example, Byzantines loved to discuss the exact relationship between Jesus and God.

In the A.D. 700s, a major argument separated the Church in the Byzantine Empire. The argument was over the use of **icons.** Icons are pictures or images of Jesus, Mary (the mother of Jesus), and the saints, or Christian holy people. Many people put them all over the walls of their churches. A few important icons were even believed to work miracles.

Some Byzantines wanted to end the use of icons. They believed that people were worshiping the icons as idols or false gods. People who supported icons believed that they were symbols of God in daily life. They also felt that icons helped explain Christianity to people.

Emperor Leo III did not agree with icons. In A.D. 726, he ordered all icons to be taken out of the churches. Government officials who took the icons were known as **iconoclasts,** or image breakers. We use this word today to mean "someone who attacks traditional beliefs or institutions."

Most Byzantines, many church leaders, and even the pope in Rome disagreed with the emperor's order. In fact, the argument over icons ruined the relationship between the churches of Rome and Constantinople. Over the next 100 years, the argument died down, and the use of icons returned. They are still an important part of Eastern Orthodox religious practice.

Conflicts Between Churches Icons were not the only reason for arguments between the churches of Constantinople and Rome. The most serious argument was about how churches should be organized. The pope said that he was the head of all the Christian churches. The Byzantines did not agree with this. They believed the patriarch of Constantinople and other bishops were equal to the pope.

Also, sometimes one church would not help the other when they were attacked from outside. This only made problems worse. In the late A.D. 700s when Italy was invaded, the Byzantine emperor refused to help the pope. So, the pope asked a Germanic group called the Franks to help. The Franks were Roman Catholics and loyal to the pope.

The pope was thankful to the Franks for stopping the invasion. In A.D. 800, he gave the Frankish king, Charlemagne, the title of emperor. This made the Byzantines angry. They felt the leader of the Byzantines was the only true Roman emperor.

This conflict showed the different ways that the churches dealt with the government. In the Byzantine Empire, the emperor was in control, and church leaders

READING ESSENTIALS AND STUDY GUIDE 11-3 (continued)

respected his ideas. In Rome, however, the pope claimed both spiritual and political power. He often argued with kings over church and government matters.

Finally, after hundreds of years of strain, the pope and the leader of Constantinople made a huge decision. In A.D. 1054, they **excommunicated** each other. This means they stated that the other group did not belong to the church anymore. This began a **schism,** or separation, of the two most important branches of Christianity. The split between the Roman Catholic and Eastern Orthodox Churches has lasted to this day.

4. Why did Byzantines place the authority for the government and for the church in one person?

_____

_____

Christian Ideas Spread (pages 518–521)

Main Idea Christians founded new communities and spread their faith to various parts of Europe.

After the fall of Rome, the people of Western Europe were confused. Christianity helped them find the order and unity they wanted. It spread quickly into what used to be parts of the Roman Empire. It also brought new ways of thinking and living to these areas.

What Are Monasteries? During the A.D. 300s, a new kind of religious group formed in the Eastern Roman Empire. Men called monks lived together in religious communities called **monasteries.** Monasteries were built near cities and in far away areas.

Anthony was one of the earliest monks. He organized a monastery in the deserts of Egypt. Monks tried to live a spiritual life away from the temptations of the world. Many also tried to do good deeds and be examples of how Christians should live. Women soon followed the monks' example and created groups of their own. These women were called nuns, and they lived in convents.

In the early A.D. 400s, a Roman woman named Paula built churches, a hospital, and a convent. When her husband died, she gave up her money and went to Palestine. She also helped a scholar named Jerome rewrite the Hebrew and Greek Bible in Latin.

A bishop called Basil wrote a list of rules for monks and nuns to follow. This list, called the Basilian Rule, became the guide for Eastern Orthodox religious life.

In the West, an Italian monk named Benedict wrote another set of rules for monks. Monks who followed the Benedictine Rule gave up their belongings, lived simply, and spent their time in work and prayer. Like Basil's rule in the East, Benedict's rule became the standard for monks and nuns in the West. Basilian and Benedictine communities are still around today.

Monks and nuns began to play important roles in Roman Catholic and Eastern Orthodox life. They ran hospitals and schools, and helped the poor. They also helped protect Greek and Roman writings. One important job was to be **missionaries.** Missionaries teach their religion to those who do not believe.

Christianity Spreads North Two brothers, Cyril and Methodius, were very successful Byzantine missionaries. They brought Christian teachings to people in Eastern Europe called the Slavs.

About A.D. 863, Cyril invented a new alphabet. He wanted the Christian message to be in the Slavic languages. He believed that people would be more interested in Christianity if they could worship and read the Bible in their own languages. He based the Cyrillic alphabet on Greek letters. It is still used today by Russians, Ukrainians, Serbs, and Bulgarians.

Eastern Orthodox missionaries traveled in northern lands that bordered the Byzantine Empire. At the same time, other missionaries from Rome were also busy.

READING ESSENTIALS AND STUDY GUIDE 11-3 (continued)

Christianity Spreads West In the West, Christian missionaries looked to the islands of Britain and Ireland. In the A.D. 300s, Roman soldiers that were in Britain were called back to Rome to fight against Germanic invaders. When they left, Britain was opened to attack by others.

Starting in the A.D. 400s, Britain was invaded by tribes from what are today known as Germany and Denmark. These people were the Angles and the Saxons. They came together as the Anglo-Saxons. They built communities and set up several small kingdoms. The southern part of Britain soon became known as Angleland, or England.

While invading Britain, the Angles and Saxons pushed out the people already living there. These people were called the Celts. Some Celts fled to the mountains of Britain. Others went to Ireland.

A priest named Patrick brought Christianity to Ireland. He set up a lot of monasteries and churches. Over the next centuries, Irish monks played an important role in protecting Christian and Roman learning.

The Anglo-Saxon kingdoms of Britain were slower than Ireland to accept Christianity. In A.D. 567, Pope Gregory I sent about 40 monks from Rome to take Christianity to England.

The missionaries persuaded Ethelbert, the ruler of the English kingdom of Kent, to believe in Christianity. Ethelbert allowed the missionaries to build a church in his capital city of Canterbury. In about 100 years, most of England was Christian. Today, Canterbury is still an important center of Christianity in England.

5. Why were people open to Christianity after the fall of Rome?

_____

_____